AF228423

The Wells of Salvation Opened

The Wells of Salvation Opened

A Treatise Discovering the Nature, Preciousness,
Usefulness of Gospel Promises,
and Rules for the Right Application of Them

William Spurstowe

Edited by
Randall J. Pederson

Soli Deo Gloria Publications
An imprint of Reformation Heritage Books
Grand Rapids, Michigan

Soli Deo Gloria Publications
An imprint of Reformation Heritage Books
3070 29th St. SE
Grand Rapids, MI 49512
616-977-0889
orders@heritagebooks.org
www.heritagebooks.org

Printed in the United States of America
24 25 26 27 28/10 9 8 7 6 5 4 3 2

Library of Congress Cataloging-in-Publication Data

Names: Spurstowe, William, 1605?-1666, author. | Pederson, Randall J., 1975- editor.
Title: The wells of salvation opened : a treatise discovering the nature, preciousness, usefulness of gospel promises, and rules for the right application of them / William Spurstowe ; edited by Randall J. Pederson.
Description: Grand Rapids, Michigan : Soli Deo Gloria Publications, an imprint of Reformation Heritage Books, [2023]
Identifiers: LCCN 2023007696 (print) | LCCN 2023007697 (ebook) | ISBN 9798886860191 (hardcover) | ISBN 9798886860207 (epub)
Subjects: LCSH: Promises—Religious aspects—Christianity—Early works to 1800. | Bible—Commentaries—Early works to 1800. | Christian life—Puritan authors—Early works to 1800.
Classification: LCC BS680.P68 S68 2023 (print) | LCC BS680.P68 (ebook) | DDC 231.7—dc23/eng/20230411
LC record available at https://lccn.loc.gov/2023007696
LC ebook record available at https://lccn.loc.gov/2023007697

Ἀναγίνωσκε ουν ινα γινωσκης, ει δε γινωσκειν ου βουλει μη αναγινωσκε ινα μη καταγινωσκη

"Therefore, read that you may understand, but if you do not want to understand, do not read, lest you be condemned."
— Isidore of Pelusium

CONTENTS

EDITOR'S PREFACE

In the first printing of William Spurstowe's *The Wells of Salvation Opened*, the printers included a frontispiece that said simply, "Dr. Spurstowe on the Promises."[1] This gesture not only reflects the high esteem in which Spurstowe's works were held in the seventeenth century, but also speaks to his reputation as a minister, scholar, and teacher of the Bible. In fact, at that time, praise for Spurstowe's gifts and writings were common. Richard Baxter, pastor at Kidderminster and a revered divine, who knew Spurstowe personally and was a close friend, wrote that Spurstowe was "an ancient, calm, and reverend Minister."[2] Simeon Ashe, another divine who knew Spurstowe well and preached the funeral sermon of Spurstowe's only child, spoke of the religious education and godly atmosphere in the Spurstowe home.[3] Thomas Smith of Glasgow, in his *Select Memoirs*, wrote that Spurstowe was "eminently distinguished for his

---

1. William Spurstowe, *The Wells of Salvation Opened; Or, Discovering the Nature, Preciousness, Usefulness of Gospel-Promises, and Rules for the Right Application of Them* (London, 1655), sig. A2. The frontispiece was not included in the second edition of 1659.

2. Richard Baxter, *Reliquiae Baxterianae*, Vol. 2 (Oxford: Oxford University Press, 2020), 454.

3. Simeon Ashe, *Christ the Riches of the Gospel, and the Hope of Christians: A Sermon Preached at the Funeral of Mr. William Spurstowe, the only Child of Dr. Spurstowe at Hackney near London, March 10* (London, 1654), 35–38. Spurstowe's child died in his ninth year. Shortly before his death, when asked if he would wish to live

great learning, humility, charity, a cheerful temper, and a pleasant conversation."[4]

Originally published as a small quarto book, *The Wells of Salvation Opened* discusses what God's promises are, how they are to be properly used, the dangers associated with abusing them, and ultimately, how believers can find comfort in them, both in life and at the moment of death. Spurstowe was not alone in writing on the promises,[5] but his work was well regarded and much sought after;[6] in fact, numerous divines and lay readers throughout the century profited from a deep and meditative reflection on its teachings.[7]

It may be helpful for the reader to know a little about Spurstowe himself. He was an ejected minister, the son of William Spurstowe Sr. He attended Emmanuel College, Cambridge, and St. Catherine's College, for his BA and MA, and eventually earned his DD. Along with four other ministers, Spurstowe co-authored the anti-episcopal tract *Smectymnuus* in 1641.[8] He was also invited to

---

longer, Spurstowe's child answered, "I would live, that I might glorify God, and be a comfort to my father and mother."

4. Thomas Smith, *Select Memoirs of the Lives, Labors, and Sufferings of Those Pious and Learned English and Scottish Divines* (Glasgow, 1828), 598. Cp. James Reid, *Memoirs of the Lives and Writings of those Eminent Divines, who Convened at the Famous Assembly at Westminster in the Seventeenth Century* (Paisley, 1811), 1:148–51.

5. See, for instance, Vavasor Powell, *Christ and Moses Excellency, or Sion and Sinai's Glory, Being a Triplex Treatise, Distinguishing and Explaining the Two Covenants or the Gospel and the Law: And Directing to the Right Understanding, Applying, and Finding of the Informing and Assuring Promises that Belong to Both Covenants* (London, 1650); and Edward Leigh, *A Treatise of the Divine Promises in Five Books* (London, 1641).

6. *The Wells of Salvation Opened* went through at least three printings in the seventeenth century (1655, 1659, 1666).

7. For example, Edward Reynolds recommends Spurstowe on the promises in his *Imitation and Caution for Christian Women* (London, 1659), 16; and Edward Polhill cites it in *Precious Faith Considered in Its Nature, Working, and Growth* (London, 1675), 222. An Arminian bishop, Laurence Womock, thought it worthy enough to address in confrontation of Calvinism (Cf. Womock, *The Result of False Principles* [London, 1661]).

8. The tract, which sought to reprove and correct practices introduced into

and served as a member of the Westminster Assembly, took part in its debates, and along with his co-authors took the Solemn League and Covenant.

Spurstowe was an active preacher before Parliament and preached several parliamentary fast and thanksgiving sermons, including a commemoration of the Gunpowder Plot on November 5, 1644. Sometime in 1644, he also married a woman named Sarah, though nothing is known about her family history or lineage.[9]

In 1645, Spurstowe became the pastor of a parish in Hackney, a borough of London, and served on a classis with Thomas Manton. Spurstowe opposed the trial and execution of Charles I, and eventually resigned from an honorary academic position on account of his Presbyterian convictions.[10] However, in the 1650s, he reconciled with Oliver Cromwell and eventually supported Cromwell's son, Richard. Near the time of the collapse of the Interregnum, Spurstowe preached a sermon in favor of Charles II's restoration and went on delegation with Edmund Calamy to the Netherlands to meet with the exiled king. Spurstowe became one of Charles II's Presbyterian chaplains, and on at least one occasion preached before the king.

Spurstowe was also involved in the Savoy Conference in 1661, which sought to reconcile Episcopalian and Presbyterian ministers over the Book of Common Prayer, but the conference ultimately failed, and not long after an Act of Uniformity took effect in August

---

the liturgy of the English Church, was authored by Stephen Marshall, Edmund Calamy, Thomas Young, Matthew Newcomen, and William Spurstowe, with the initials of each author comprising the tract's title. John Milton, a well-known Independent, wrote in favor of the tract, while those in favor of the establishment strongly opposed it. Cf. Elliot Vernon, *London Presbyterians and the British Revolutions, 1638–64* (Manchester: Manchester University Press, 2021), ch. 2.

9. In 1669, three years after Spurstowe's death, Sarah married Anthony Tuckney, a noted Puritan theologian and professor of divinity at Cambridge.

10. Kirsteen M. Mackenzie, *The Solemn League and Covenant of the Three Kingdoms and the Commonwealth Union, 1643–1663* (Oxfordshire: Routledge, 2017).

1662, which deprived nonconforming ministers of their pastoral posts. Spurstowe thus resigned his position at the church in Hackney and spent his remaining years in retirement, in conversing with other divines, and in writing a few noteworthy tracts, *The Spiritual Chymist* (1666) and *The Wiles of Satan* (1666).

In his last years, Spurstowe established six almshouses for poor widows at Hackney, houses that were in service from 1666 to 1966.[11] After surviving the plague that swept through London in 1665, Spurstowe died suddenly in Hackney in 1666.

This edition of *Wells of Salvation Opened* has been only slightly edited. The text has been painstakingly compared to the original, with the intent to produce a faithful, and yet more accessible, text for the modern reader. Thus, archaic language has been updated spelling-wise, and short definitions to antiquated words have been added in footnotes. While Spurstowe, for the most part, used the KJV, the edition he cited from had different spelling and punctuation; thus, biblical citations have been standardized to modern printings. In the greater text, pronouns for God were capitalized, and commas have been inserted in places to help with reading. With few exceptions, I have opted to retain Spurstowe's British mixing of "which" and "that." I have also included biographical notes to aid historical context, but have purposely kept them to a minimum, so as not to draw away from the main text. Chapter titles and headings have been revised, opting for a simpler and more consistent pattern, which it is hoped will make reading the book more pleasant. An analytical overview of Spurstowe's work has been compiled to aid the reader in utilizing the text, as well as to get a sense of its overall structure.

Editing early modern books, and reprinting them in a slightly revised format, make the inaccessible accessible. And yet, whenever

---

11. In 1966, the residents of the almshouses moved to newly built houses called Dr. William Spurstowe House, which contains sixteen apartments and accommodates both men and women of the lower classes.

an editor faces the task of editing, there are always unique challenges to each text. For Spurstowe, the challenge was what to do with his use of the Greek and Latin languages. At times, they were so interwoven into the text that to remove them would seem to compromise what Spurstowe had intended. So rather than remove the languages entirely, which would be appropriate for a fully modernized or abridged text, it seemed prudent to drop them into footnotes in the places where they occurred. Readers familiar with Greek and Latin will make sense of their meaning, and readers unfamiliar with them will lose little, as Spurstowe usually translated their meaning in the text. Thus, to avoid redundancy, I have not included additional English translations in the footnotes.

While editing *The Wells of Salvation Opened*, I often got caught up in what Spurstowe was saying and forgot I was editing. He frequently draws the reader's attention to the brevity and gravity of life, that we are but pilgrims and strangers in a strange land, and that this world is not our home. We are foolish to lose sight of its temporary and transient nature. Ultimately, we must draw our attention heavenward and make frequent use of the promises; in doing so, we will find the God who promises to be faithful and true.

For me, editing Spurstowe was not a scholarly exercise as much as it was a devotional one. My first exposure to *The Wells of Salvation Opened* was over twenty years ago when I introduced a facsimile reprint. I have never lost an appreciation for the work or the impact it had on my mind. I am grateful for the opportunity to revisit Spurstowe and pray that this new edition will make it into even more hands, that old and new readers of Spurstowe will draw deep from his *Wells of Salvation* and find in it refreshing and enlivening springs. Finally, it is hoped that by God's grace it will become a staple in households and will foster the pleading of God's promises back to Him.

ANALYTICAL OVERVIEW

2 Peter 1:4 and God's Promises

Text — Whereby [or by whom] are given unto us exceeding great and precious promises: that by these ye might be partakers of the divine nature, having escaped the corruption that is in the world through lust (chapter 1).

What a Promise Is

Definition — A promise is a declaration of God's will wherein He signifies what particular good things He will freely bestow and the evils that He will remove (chapter 2).

The Greatness and Preciousness of the Promises

Excellency 1 — Promises are rooted in and spring from our precious Christ (chapter 3).

Excellency 2 — Promises are the root of the most excellent and noble grace of faith (chapter 3).

Excellency 3 — Promises give us right and title to things of remarkable worth and value (chapter 3).

Excellency 4 — Promises have the noble effects of making us partakers of the divine nature (chapter 4).

Excellency 5 — Promises are grounds of matchless consolation (chapter 5).

Rules for Rightly Using the Promises

Positive Rule 1 — Eye God in the promises (chapter 6).

Positive Rule 2 — Promises of growth in grace are conditional in their performance (chapter 7).

Positive Rule 3 — Promises depend on one another, and their fixed order must not be broken or inverted (chapter 7).

Positive Rule 4 — Meditate thoroughly and frequently on the promises (chapter 7).

Positive Rule 5 — Be much in the use and application of the promises (chapter 7).

Positive Rule 6 — Continue in a holy waiting upon God until the promises are fulfilled (chapter 8).

Positive Rule 7 — Make choice of some special promises to resort to in extremity (chapter 8).

Positive Rule 8 — Consider biblical examples to whom promises have been fulfilled (chapter 8).

Positive Rule 9 — Preserve communion with and dependence on the Holy Spirit (chapter 8).

Positive Rule 10 — Be truly thankful for the least dawnings of mercy which the promises have afforded (chapter 8).

Cautionary Rule 1 — Take heed of resting in a general faith of assent (chapter 9).

Cautionary Rule 2 — Take heed of poring too much on the measure and degrees of humiliation (chapter 9).

Cautionary Rule 3 — Take heed of observing and eyeing the providences of God above His promises (chapter 10).

Cautionary Rule 4 — Take heed of a sinful and affected curiosity in selecting promises (chapter 10).

Cautionary Rule 5 — Take heed of carnal reasoning (chapter 10).

Cautionary Rule 6 — Take heed of groundless fancies concerning the manner of receiving comfort from the promises (chapter 11).

Cautionary Rule 7 — Take heed of setting your heart on earthly objects (chapter 11).

Useful Queries and Cases Concerning the Promises

Query 1 — Does the essence of saving faith lie in a prevailing assurance of one's faith in Christ (chapter 12)?

Query 2 — What use may a believer make of the promises of mercy and pardon after relapses into gross sin (chapter 13)?

Query 3 — What use may a believer make of the promises for future ages that he cannot expect to see (chapter 14)?

Query 4 — Do believers who make diligent use of the promises always enjoy the comfort of assurance in death (chapter 15)?

Query 5 — What use may believers make of promises of temporal blessings (chapter 16)?

Practical Inferences and Applications from the Doctrine of the Promises

Application 1 — It is a horrible sin to neglect or abuse the promises (chapter 17).

Application 2 — There are wide differences between the promises of God and Satan (chapter 18).

Application 3 — The worst estate of believers is better than the best estate of an unbeliever (chapter 19).

Application 4 — Believers should abound in all thankfulness to God for being partakers of such precious promises (chapter 20).

Application 5 — Believers should act faith in the precious promises (chapter 21).

Dr. Spurstowe on the Promises

EPISTLE DEDICATORY

To the Right Honorable Edward,
Earl of Manchester, Viscount Mandeville,
Baron of Kimbolton[1]

Right Honorable,

There are two ranks of men extremely differing in regard of their estate and condition that use for the most part to go with staves[2] in their hands but not to the same end or purpose. The nobleman carries his as a badge and emblem of his office and high honor, it being an ancient custom for princes to give the investiture[3] into places of dignity and eminence by the delivering of a staff.[4] The common traveler takes up his the better to support him in the length of his journey, and to ease him in the difficulty and roughness of the way. But these staves of honor God has cut asunder as He did those of beauty and bands (Zech. 11:7), having had for these late years a sharp contest with the cedars of the land, and which is a lamentation, and shall be for a lamentation, has dried up the roots from whence they sprang.

That which I presume to put into your Honor's hand is the staff of a traveler, yet not of such a one as beats the common road and

---

1. Edward Montagu (1602–1671), 2nd Earl of Manchester, was a Parliamentarian General in the English Civil Wars, and was, for a time, Oliver Cromwell's commanding officer. In 1649, he opposed the trial and execution of Charles I, and retired from public life during the Commonwealth. He resumed political activity when Charles II was restored to the English throne and was appointed General in the royal army in 1667.

2. *staves*: long pole, wooden stick, or staff.

3. *investiture*: ceremoniously dressing a bishop or prelate with vestments, ring, crozier, etc.

4. *per traditionem baculi.*

path of the world, but of such who professing themselves strangers and sojourners on earth both seek and mind a heavenly country, and to be among the number of those (I am persuaded) you do not only count it your duty but also make it your work, esteeming it a greater glory to be one of Zion's pilgrims than of England's peers. Now how expedient and necessary a staff is in this journey, I would the times themselves did not abundantly speak; the difficulties of which have been such as that to many religion itself has become a stone of stumbling and a rock of offense. Others as dejected have fainted in their profession and have cast away their confidence for want of looking up unto the promises, which in such seasons are the believer's only support and assurance, that though the way of the Lamb be a way of blood, yet the end is a throne of glory and a crown of life. That I may, therefore, strengthen your hands in God and be serviceable to your faith, I have made bold to dedicate this small treatise of the promises to your Honor, which I wish might prove in your hands as the rod of myrtle in the hand of the traveler, which as historians report keeps him from growing weary. And that it might so tend to the increase of spiritual strength, as that when the youths shall faint and the young men utterly fall, you may be as those that wait upon God, who run and are not weary, and walk and are not faint (Isa. 40:31). However, though I can communicate no virtue unto it, yet I shall not cease to follow it with my prayers, beseeching God that both it and all other means which through His grace you may enjoy for the welfare of your soul, may prove so successful by His blessings as that you may reap the rich fruit of all the promises in the everlasting fruition of life and glory. And that your noble posterity may be heirs also together with yourself of the same mercies. So I rest,

Your Honors in all Christian Observance,
William Spurstowe
October 26, 1654

CHRISTIAN READER

There is a vanity with which prefaces are tainted, not much unlike that predominant folly in these days of wantonness of spotting of faces; for as some industriously place artificial spots here and there, which by their contrariety may serve as a foil to their beauty and heighten it to the lust and fancy of others beyond what it is in truth, so others by a severe observance and calculation of the omissions and failings of such who have treated the same or like subject with themselves, by presenting them to the reader's view, make use of their defects as so many beauty spots to enamor him the more with the absolute completeness of their books. But far be it from me to make the profitable pains of those who have employed their time and busied their thoughts on such a noble subject as the promises are to serve as a dark shadow to set off this small treatise concerning them, which I now put into your hands. I have reaped both light and profit from them, and therefore cannot but thankfully acknowledge it. Nor do I conceive that I have comprised the great worth of the promises in this manual as he of old did Homer's Iliads in a nutshell; or to have done that which may be a bar to the labors of others whose abilities are greater and more fit to come under a public view than mine are. The promises are a large field in which the wise merchant may find more pearls hidden than are yet espied, a rich mine in which the diligent laborer may dig forth more fine gold than any yet have taken from them. They are the church's storehouse while it is on this side of heaven, from whence believers in all ages may be filled with comfort, as every eye is with new light that beholds the sun. So that there is still a great opportunity for the ministers of God to put their sickle into this harvest, and an encouragement also to believers to take hold of all helps and advantages that may be afforded them for the clearing of their knowledge, and the quickening of their affections, in the daily use and application of the promises. And if to either, or both of these ends, this small tract (which is the substance of sundry sermons preached divers years past) may in the least conduce, I shall seek no other recompense from you than that I may have an interest in your prayers, both for an increase of grace and of abilities whereby I may be made more serviceable to the glory of His name unto whom all ought to live. So I rest,

Yours to serve you in Christ,
William Spurstowe
Hackney, October 26, 1654

CHAPTER 1

The Text Opened and the Particulars Proposed

Whereby [or by whom] are given unto us exceeding great and precious promises: that by these ye might be partakers of the divine nature, having escaped the corruption that is in the world through lust.

—2 PETER 1:4

The natural life of man is usually divided into the three states of childhood, youth, and old age, unto which St. John aptly alluding makes the same distinction of the spiritual life of believers, whom he ranks into children, young men, and fathers. [He ranks them] into children for their tenderness and weakness, into young men for their strength and confidence, into fathers for their knowledge and experience in the high mysteries of the gospel. All which though differing in regard of their condition, do yet agree in the principle from whence their life is derived, and in the means by which it is carried on and preserved. The principle of every believer's life is Christ, and the means of its preservation are the promises whose virtue and efficacy is such as happily suits itself with the several ages and conditions of believers. The promises are the babe's milk by which they are nourished, the full breasts from whence they suck both grace and comfort. They are the young men's evidences by which they are animated to combat with the wicked one, and assured of being crowned with victory over him. They are the old men's staff, upon the top of which, like aged Jacob, they may safely lean and worship God, it being a staff for power like Moses's rod, and for flourishing like Aaron's, budding, blossoming, and yielding precious fruit. So that it is of more than ordinary concernment unto every one of them that look upon themselves as believers (whatsoever pitch and stature they have arrived unto) not to be supine[1] and careless in the frequent use and due application of the promises, which from their implantation into Christ to their full enjoyment of Him are the chief aids and support both of life and growth. Nor are they to be like unskillful lapidaries,[2] little valuing the worth of such oriental pearls, which are the only riches and treasure of every heir of glory on this side of heaven. Concerning which this verse holds forth sundry weighty particulars, branching itself out into as many parts as that river that went out of Eden to water the garden, "from thence it was parted, and became into four heads" (Gen. 2:10).

The Source of Promises

The first is the fountain from whence the promises flow, to which (if we read the words "by whom"[3]) the relative particle fairly guides us as standing mercury does the doubtful traveler. Expositors about the reading of the words do somewhat differ, but not jar, which the variety of lections[4] both in the Greek and Latin copies have chiefly occasioned. Some read "whereby,"[5] and so connecting this verse with the former would have the

---

1. *supine:* lazy.

2. *lapidary:* someone who is skilled in the nature and kinds of gems or precious stones.

3. *per quem.*

4. *lection:* reading or interpretation.

5. δι᾽ ὧν.

sense to run thus: "Through the knowledge of him that hath called us by glory and virtue, whereby are given unto us," etc. Prosper,[6] as also Bede,[7] reads "by which";[8] that is, knowledge of God are given unto us exceeding great and precious promises; from whence he makes this collection, "The more perfectly any man knows God, the more fully sensible he is of the transcendent worth of His promises."[9] Others again conceive the most genuine lection of the verse (though haply the less frequent) to be "by whom"[10] rather than "whereby."[11] And that [is] because, as Estius[12] observes, it renders the sense most evangelical and gospel-like;[13] [that is,] it points out Christ unto us, who is the Alpha and Omega of all the promises, the only Original from whence they spring and the center in which they meet. To Him they were all first made and ratified on our behalf; in Him they are all fulfilled and accomplished unto us. As the rivers have their efflux from the sea, and their reflux into the sea, so have the promises their emanation from Christ, their revolution into Christ. They flow freely from Him; they lead sweetly to Him.

The Gift of Promises

The second branch is the tenure and manner of interest that believers have in the promises. They are given unto us. In propriety of language, promises are rather made than given; but

---

6. Prosper of Aquitaine (ca. 390–ca. 455), a disciple and defender of Augustine of Hippo.

7. Bede (673/4–735), a scholar of the Anglo-Saxon period, also known as the father of English history for his *Ecclesiastical History of the English People*.

8. *per quam.*

9. *Qud quis perfectius Deum cognoscit, tanto altius promissorum ejus magnitudinem sentiat.*

10. δὶ ὦ.

11. δὶ ὦν.

12. Estius (1542–1613), or Willem Hessels van Est, a Dutch Roman Catholic exegete and commentator, known for his comments on the Pauline Epistles.

13. *prabet sensum maxime Evangelicum.*

by a metonymy[14] usual in Scripture, they are put for the things promised, the blessings both of grace and glory. All which though purchased by Christ with the price of His blood are yet conferred and freely bestowed upon believers by His mercy. The hidden manna, a type of our heavenly consolations, the white stone, the emblem of our perfect justification, the new name, the earnest of our adoption in glory, they are all favors not set to sell but given (Rev. 2:17). Out of the full heap, Christ invites us not to buy but to take, and the penniless are the most welcome (Isa. 55:1). "Grace," says Bernard,[15] "is freely given, yea, when it is bought, it is bought freely and without price."[16]

The Value of Promises

The third is the goodness and worth of the promises set forth by a double character: "exceedingly great and precious." Greatness and goodness are then most refulgent[17] when they meet in the same subject, and are joined by natural couples and connections, like the curtains of the Tabernacle that were looped one to another. But such a conjunction as it is glorious, so it is rare, and seldom found either in persons or in things. In persons, they are so dissociated, as if they were of lineages altogether distinct and had small or no affinity. Rarely are great men good or good men great. And as in persons, so in things they are not often linked and chained together. Pebbles are great, but not precious. Pearls are precious, but not great. Water in the sea is abundant, but not pure; in the brook, it is pure but not abundant. But, in

---

14. *metonymy*: a figure of speech in which a thing or concept is referred to by the name of something closely associated with it.

15. Bernard of Clairvaux (1090–1153), an abbot and medieval mystic whose writings had a profound impact of medieval church life and culture, as well as the Protestant Reformation.

16. *Gratia gratis datur, etiam cum emitur, gratis emitur.*

17. *refulgent*: radiant, resplendent, shining with a brilliant light.

the promises, there is a full and happy concurrence of both. They are made up of things wherein greatness and worth vie with each other. Everlasting life is as sweet as it is long; heaven is as glorious in its beauty as it is vast in its dimensions. The crown of righteousness that is laid up is as rich as weighty. There is no one promise of the gospel but is of that extent for its latitude and of that value for its preciousness that he deserves to be eternally poor who having that for his subsistence looks upon any man who has an interest in none greater or richer than himself, though the gravel of the river was turned into pearls, and every shower of rain from the clouds into a shower of silver and gold to supply his wants.

The Purpose of Promises

The fourth particular is the high and noble end of the donation of the promises: "That by them we might be partakers of the divine nature." Painters, when they picture angels, do not intend similitude but beauty. Nor does the apostle in this expression aim at any essential change and conversion of our substance into the nature of God and Christ, but only at the elevation and dignifying of our nature by Christ. Our near union with Him restores us to a higher similitude and likeness of God than ever we attained in our primitive perfection; but it does not introduce any real transmutation either of our bodies or souls into the divine nature. For if that stupendous union of the two natures in one person, the Lord Christ, does not effect an essential change in either, but that both natures conserve and retain their distinct properties without mixture or confusion, much less can the union between Christ and believers, which is not a personal union, but a union of persons made by the Spirit and by faith, cause any such alteration as that our nature, losing its own subsistence, should wholly pass into the divine and be swallowed up in the abyss of it, as a drop of rain does when it falls into the wide ocean. Pithily does Cyprian[18] express this truth when he affirms, "Ours and Christ's conjunction neither mingles persons nor unites substances but conjoins our affections and bring into a league of amity our wills."[19] [This is] suitable to that of the apostle, "But he that is joined unto the Lord is one spirit" (1 Cor. 6:17).

---

18. Cyprian (ca. 210–258), Bishop of Carthage and early Christian writer.

19. This saying is taken from the work *De Coena Domini* (On the Lord's Supper), a Latin text commonly attributed to Cyprian in the seventeenth century. However, modern scholarship identifies the work as belonging to the medieval writer Eernaldus Bonaevallis. See Nicholas Thompson, *Eucharistic Sacrifice and Patristic Tradition in the Theology of Martin Bucer, 1534–1546* (Leiden: Brill, 2004), 76.

CHAPTER 2

What a Promise Is

It is not designed by me as the subject of my present task to undertake a distinct and full prosecution[1] of all these four particulars in the text, every one of which, like gold in the beating, would easily diffuse and spread themselves into a large compass, but occasionally to glance at them as they conduce to the illustration of that heading and branch that I shall single and cull out from the rest as the present subject upon which I shall pitch and fix my thoughts, and that is the matchless worth and goodness of the promises of the gospel. It is a truth of much weight and sweetness to every believer, but yet, as it lies contracted in a proposition, it does not reveal so much of it as when drawn forth into a full explication. [They are] like colors that are less beautiful and pleasing while they lie on the palette of the painter than when placed and spread on the picture by the pencil of the artificer. I shall, therefore, in the unfolding of it endeavor these five things:

First, to show what a promise is (chapter 2).

Secondly, [show] in what respects they are great and precious (chapters 3–5).

---

1. *prosecution*: detailed study.

Thirdly, give rules about the due application of them (chapters 6–11).

Fourthly, resolve some useful queries and cases concerning them (chapters 12–16).

Fifthly, close and shut up all with some practical inferences and genuine applications such as flow from the doctrine of the promises. The honey which drops from the comb is of all the best and sweetest (chapters 17–21).

First, what a promise is. It is a declaration of God's will wherein He signifies what particular good things He will freely bestow and the evils that He will remove. This description, like the box of spikenard in the gospel, may be more useful when it is broken than whole. I shall, therefore, take it into pieces and give an account of it in the several parcels.

A Declaration of God's Will

First, a promise is a declaration of God's will, it being a kind of middle thing between His purpose and performance, His intension[2] of good and the execution of it upon those whom He loves. And as wicked Jezebel could not satisfy her hatred of Elijah the prophet in intending evil unto him, and effecting it upon him in time as she could, but withal she let fall a heavy threatening against him, strengthened with a bitter imprecation upon herself, as an obliging tie to put in execution the designed evil: "So let the gods do to me, and more also, if I make not thy life as the life of one of them by to morrow about this time" (1 Kings 19:2). So much less can the love of God satisfy itself in a gracious decree and purpose of good towards His elect shut up in His own breast, and the actual performance of it in the fullness of time unless withal He discloses it unto them beforehand

---

2. *intension*: resolution, determination.

both as a ground of present comfort in the knowledge thereof and of hope and expectation in the certain enjoyment of the good things promised hereafter. God also confirming the Word of His truth by an oath, not for any necessity or weakness in itself, but out of superabundant love unto the heirs of promise: "That by two immutable things, in which it was impossible for God to lie, we might have a strong consolation" (Heb. 6:18).

Signifies Good Things

Secondly, it is a declaration concerning good. And thereby a promise is differenced from the threatenings of God, which in divers respects have a near affinity with His promises. For they, as things of a middle nature, intervene between the decree of His wrath and the execution of it; they are let fall in the Word as so many discoveries of God's anger against sin and set as powerful stops to check and bound the lusts of sinners who are apt to dash themselves against the rock of divine displeasure. They are sealed with the same oath of God with which the promises are ratified so that they might be as full of dread to sinners in the expectation of the fulfilling of them as the promises are of comfort to believers.

Freely Bestowed

Thirdly, it concerns good things freely bestowed. And thereby it is distinguished from the commands that are also significations of God's will concerning good. But it is of the good of duty enjoined to be done, not of the good of mercy to be received. The precepts of God and the promises of God always go together in the Word, as the veins and the arteries do in the body. Wherever there is a vein that carries blood, there also accompanies it an artery that carries spirits.[3] So, wherever there is a precept in the

---

3. *spirits*: life, energy.

Word that enjoins duty, there also is an answerable promise that assures comfort. The one holds forth the good to be done, the other the good to be received.

Particular Good Things

Fourthly, it is of particular good things. And this may serve to hint and point out one considerable difference between the covenant of grace and the promises. The covenant is the entire vintage of the heavenly Canaan; and the promises are as the several clusters of blessing; that is, [they are] as a glorious constellation of many celestial bodies in the firmament of the Scriptures. And they are as so many single stars shining in their proper orbs; that is, [they are] as the total sum in the inventory of a believer's estate; and they are as the distinct particulars that make it up. All the sweetness, beauty, and worth that are diffused throughout the promises are collected in the covenant, as the scattered light in the creation was into the body of the sun. God's stipulation of becoming ours, and of making us to be His (Jer. 31:33), comprises everything that is desirable, from the first of goods to the last, and is both the basis and the spire, the cornerstone and the top-stone of every Christian's happiness.

Evils Removed

Fifthly, and last, is added the evils that He will remove. And this takes in all the privative mercies and blessings that the promises of the gospel hold forth to believers which, though they are not the resplendent part of their happiness, are yet of so necessary a concurrence unto it that without them it can never be absolute or entire. True happiness consists of a double branch, of an immunity or freedom from evils and the enjoyment of good, both [of] which are tacitly couched in every promise, but in many most expressly and fully set down, "For the LORD God is a sun and shield: the LORD will give grace and glory: no good thing will he withhold from them that walk uprightly" (Ps. 84:11). [He is] a sun to give life and a shield to preserve life given, a sun to make fruitful in all good, and a shield to protect from all danger. [In] Isaiah 25:6–8, the felicity of the church is described by a feast of fat things full of marrow, of wines on the lees well refined that the Lord will make unto His people in Mount Zion. But to render these dainties the more pleasing, He promises also to take away the face of the covering, to swallow up death in victory, and to wipe away all tears from their eyes. Blindness that may hinder the clear knowledge, death that may interrupt the perpetuity, sorrow that may diminish the sweetness of this blessed estate, shall all by a powerful hand be removed and done away.

CHAPTER 3

The Excellency and Preciousness of the Promises

Having shown what a promise is, the second thing that falls under consideration is the great worth and excellence of the promises, which in divers respects will appear to be such if compared with the choicest of earthly comforts. The one will be as a sovereign elixir full of spirits, and the other as the inactive and sapless dregs. Or, if with the richest treasures of the world, the one will be as so much refined gold and the other as so much impure dross. What Job said concerning the power of God, "If I speak of strength, lo, he is strong" (Job 9:19), may truly also be said of the riches of the promises. If you speak of worth, lo, they are precious indeed.

Christ the Root of the Promises

First, the promises derive a preciousness from the root and principle from whence they spring. They are as so many beams of Christ the Sun of righteousness [Mal. 4:2] and impart a light which discovers His excellency, evidences our propriety, and affects in us a blessed purity. They are the desirable fruit of the tree of life; [they are] not of that tree of life in the beginning of the Bible, which stood in Adam's paradise on earth, but of that in the end of the Bible in Saint John's paradise in heaven, not of that which was guarded with cherubims and a flaming sword that it might not be touched, but of that in the midst of the city of God, free for every believer to put forth the hand of faith and to take and eat of the fruit of it both as food and medicine. They are the crystal streams of that river of life that proceeded out of the throne of God and the Lamb (Rev. 22:1), whose waters in time of drought never fail, but with their overflowing plenty satisfy the thirsty, [and] with their cooling virtue allay the heat of the wearied, and with their sweetness cheer and revive the drooping and dejected spirits.

And now, methinks, I cannot but make a pause and stand a while admiring both a believer's happiness and Christ's bounty, each of which are of such transcendence that they better suit with a holy wonderment than with the most lively and full expressions. Oh, how happy is every believer whose light is the love of Christ shining in the rays of the promises; whose food is the tree of life that continually yields fruit both new and various; whose cordials are the waters of life, not sparingly given to a bare sustentation, but freely flowing to a delightful satiety! Well might David, in rapture, say, "What is man that thou art mindful of him? and the son of man, that thou visitest him? For thou hast made him a little lower than the angels" (Ps. 8:4–5). And well also might Paul as one standing upon the shore and fathoming the sea of God's mercy cry out, "O the depth of the riches both of the wisdom and knowledge of God!" (Rom. 11:33). And most joyfully may every heir of the promise say, "The lines are fallen unto me in pleasant places; yea, I have a goodly heritage" (Ps. 16:6), to whom such precious promises are given as exceed both in glory and certainty all earthly performances whatever, being in Christ from whom they all come, "Yea," and "Amen" (2 Cor. 1:20).

The Promises Are the Root of Faith

Secondly, the promises may be said to be great and precious in respect of that proximity and peculiar relation they have to the most excellent and noble grace of faith above all other graces whatsoever. They are the precious objects of precious faith, as the apostle styles it (2 Peter 1:1). It is true that the quickening influence and virtue of the promises reach every grace of the Spirit, whereby they are both facilitated and strengthened in their several motions and operations. By them hope is kept alive in its expectation of good, patience is supported under difficulties, holiness is perfected, love is inflamed, and a blessed fear of God is preserved. But yet all this is not done by the immediate intercourse that these graces have with the promises, but by the intervention of faith that first feeds upon them as the manna of the gospel, and then communicates the sweetness and virtue that it draws and receives from them in a suitable manner to every other grace. As the root first sucks the juice and sap from the earth of which it makes a concoction, and then sends forth a digested nourishment unto the several branches, and fruit that hangs upon the tree, so does the radical grace of faith distribute to other graces that strength and life that it is partaker of from Christ and His promises. And as the concoction that faith makes is more or less perfect, so are the operations of every grace the more or less vigorous. Faith is a kind of mediator between Christ and all our graces, as Christ is between us and God. As we have nothing from God but [what] we receive by and through Christ, so no grace is partaker of any virtue and influence from Christ but by the mediation and intervention of faith.

The Things Promised Are Precious

Thirdly, the promises are exceedingly great and precious in respect of the remarkable worth and value of those things in which they interest believers and give them a right unto by an unquestionable claim and title. It is a full and weighty observation (of which Grotius[1] has afforded two parts) that there are three things that clearly demonstrate and also highly commend the doctrine of the gospel above any other religion whatever: the certainty of principles of trust, the sanctity of precepts, and the transcendence of rewards. What religion is there amongst that multiplicity which has found entertainment in the world wherein God is represented to the soul so meet and fit an object of trust as in the gospel? Majesty being there made accessible by the condescension of goodness, and God and man who were at a distance are so nearly united together in one, as that it is impossible to be determined whether be the greater wonder, the mystery or the mercy. Where are there in any religion such exact precepts of holiness enjoined as in the gospel, which by a law upon every motion of the soul and become either a rule to guide it or a judge to censure it. Or where, by search, do we find such ample and full rewards as may match and parallel the rewards of the gospel to believers? There we read of the bread of life for food, of the waters of life for pleasure and delight, of a crown of life for honor, of an inheritance in life for riches, and of a weight of glory for clothing and beauty. All which are not mentioned in the Word as in a bare and naked declaratory that conveys nothing of title or interest and speaks rather the perfection of heaven than the happiness of believers but are set down and specified in the promises that, which as they declare a goodness and excellence in things, also give a right and propriety unto persons in them. They are in the matters of God as deeds and evidences are in the matters of men, which, when they are signed, sealed, witnessed, and delivered, invest men in a just and legal right of whatever is mentioned and contained in them.

____

1. Hugo Grotius (1583–1645), Dutch humanist, lawyer, diplomat, and theologian, who studied at Leiden University, and advocated for religious toleration and natural law.

All that a believer has to plead or to show for that state of glory of which he is an heir is the promise. Eternal life is by promise: "And this is the promise that he hath promised us, even eternal life" (1 John 2:25). The crown is by promise: "He shall receive the crown of life, which the Lord hath promised to them that love him" (James 1:12). The kingdom, where for love all shall be sons, for birthright heirs, for dignity kings, is only by promise: "Hath not God chosen the poor of this world rich in faith, and heirs of the kingdom which he hath promised to them that love him?" (James 2:5). The bounty laid up and the bounty laid out, the good that a believer expects and the good that he enjoys, both flow from the promise, without which no present thing could be sweet, nor no future thing would be certain, which by the stability of the promise are now made "gifts…without repentance"[2] (Rom. 11:29). Or, as Augustine[3] expounds it, "gifts firmly fixed without change."[4] Every promise being ratified by God's oath, than which nothing is more immutable; sealed by the blood of Christ, than which nothing is more precious; testified by the Spirit, than whom nothing is more true; delivered by the hand of mercy, than which nothing is more free; and received by the hand of faith, than which nothing is more sure.

---

2. χαρίσματα αμεταμέλητα.

3. Augustine of Hippo (354–430), church father and bishop, whose writings deeply influenced Christian theology and the culture of the West.

4. *dona sine mutatione stabiliter fixa.*

CHAPTER 4

The Noble Effect of the Promises

Fourthly, the promises of the gospel are exceedingly great and precious in regard of that high and noble effect that they work in believers, who, by the energy and powerful operation of the promises, are raised to the utmost pitch both of perfection and blessedness in their being and estate, being by them made partakers of the divine nature, as the apostle tells us. This is done not by having a share and partnership in the substance and essence of God, and thereby to become drops, beams, and particles of the deity, as some have most fondly dreamed, but by a participation of divine qualities and excellences whereby believers are made conformable unto God, having those perfections that are in the holy nature of God and Christ by way of eminence to be formally, or according to the method of creation, imprinted and stamped on their souls so far as the image of His infinite holiness is expressible in a limited and restrained being. As the wax, when it receives an impression from the seal, does not participate of the essence of the seal, but only receives a signature and stamp made upon it, so when God leaves a character and print of His holiness or other excellences upon the soul, He does not communicate anything of His substance or essence but effects only a resemblance in the creature of those perfections that are truly in Himself, which being originally and totally derived from Him may in some sort be said to be the divine nature. In the painter's table, that is called a face or hand that is only the lively image or representation of such things to the eye. And so those divine lineaments of beauty and holiness that are drawn by the finger of God upon the soul of believers may be called the divine nature as they are shadowy representations of His own glorious being but not as they are any particles or traduction[1] of it. The highest honor that any creature can attain unto is to be a living picture of God, to show forth, as the apostle says (1 Peter 2:9), the virtues of God and Christ. And he that raises it any higher must have swelling and lofty thoughts of the creature, and low and dishonorable thoughts of God. Now, this likeness to God, or this *Deiformitas, Christiformitas*,[2] as the pious ancients were wont to style it, is wrought by the promises.

Words of Life

First, they are the words of Spirit and life (John 6:63). They are the immortal seed (1 Peter 1:23), whereby a man is begotten again and made partaker of a second birth, in which he bears the image of the second Adam, the Lord from heaven; as in the other, He did bear the similitude of the first Adam who was "of the earth, earthly" (1 Cor. 15:47). The promises have in them a formative virtue and power[3] to mold and fashion the heart to holiness, and to introduce the image of Christ into it, in regard of that native purity which dwells in them, and is above gold that has been seven times tried in the fire (Ps. 12:6). Therefore, our Savior tells His disciples that they were clean through the Word which He had spoken to them (John 15:3). And when He

---

1. *traduction*: transmission.

2. *Deiformitas, Christiformitas*: becoming a child of God and of imitating Christ's virtue.

3. *vim* πλασικὴν.

prayed to God to sanctify them, His prayer is, "Sanctify them through thy truth: thy word is truth" (John 17:17).

Objects of Faith and Hope

Secondly, believers may be said to be partakers of the divine nature by the promises, as they are the objects of faith and hope. Both which are graces that have in them a wonderful aptitude to cleanse and purify the subjects in which they dwell, and to introduce true holiness in which the lively image and resemblance of God chiefly consist.

1. Faith believes the truth of those things which God has promised and apprehends also the worth and excellence of them to be such that thereby it is made firm and constant in its adherence, vigorous and active in its endeavors to use all means for obtaining conformity to God and Christ, and the escaping of the corruption that is in the world through lust. For till a man comes to be a believer, he is, by the temptations of Satan and the specious promises with which they usually come attended, drawn aside to the commission of the worst of sins in which, though he wearies himself to find what first was seemingly promised, yet he meets with nothing but delusions and disappointments of his expectation. Balaam has an edge set upon his spirit to curse the people of God by a promise of preferment made unto him, and he tires himself in going from place to place to effect it; but God hinders him from doing the one and Balak denies giving to him the other. So Judas, by a bait that suits his covetousness, undertakes to sell his Lord. But when he has accomplished his wickedness and received his wages, he throws it away and dares not keep what before he so earnestly thirsted after. The blood of his Master made every piece of the silver look ghastly, so that now he sees another image upon it than Caesar's, and cries out that he had sinned in betraying innocent blood.

Now faith enables a believer to discern a snare, a defilement under all the gilded allurements of Satan and the world. And, therefore, he rejects with scorn those temptations with which others are miserably captivated, and resists with resolution all the courtings and solicitations of the flesh to which others yield, beholding only a stability and preciousness in those promises that have the oath of God to make them sure, and His love to make them sweet. And these only have a prevailing power with him to cause him so to order his conversation in all manner of holiness that he may walk as becomes an heir of heaven and an adopted son of the Most High God to walk.

2. As faith by believing the promises purifies the heart, so also does hope, which expects the performance of what faith believes, work and produce the same effects. "And every man that hath this hope in him purifieth himself, even as he is pure" (1 John 3:3). The expectation that believers have by the promises is not a supine oscitancy[4] whereby they look to be possessed of life and glory without any care or endeavors of theirs to obtain it, like to callow[5] and unfeathered birds that lie in the nest and have all their food brought to them, gaping only to receive it. But it is an expectation accompanied with diligence and industry for the fruition of what they expect. "The grace of God," says Paul, "teaching us that, denying ungodliness and worldly lusts, we should live soberly, righteously, and godly, in this present world" (Titus 2:11–12). And the ground of this he subjoins in verse 13, "Looking for that blessed hope, and the glorious appearing of the great God and our Saviour Jesus Christ." He that truly expects glory earnestly pursues grace (Heb. 12:14). He that hopes to be with God in heaven uses all means to be like God on earth. A heavenly conversation is the natural fruit of a heavenly

---

4. *oscitancy*: inattention, negligence.
5. *callow*: bald.

expectation: "For our conversation is in heaven; from whence also we look for the Saviour, the Lord Jesus Christ" (Phil. 3:20). The heathen could say that labor was the husband of hope. There is hope the harlot and hope the wife. Hope the married woman is distinguished from hope the harlot by this: she always accompanies her husband's labor. True hope looks to enjoy nothing but what is gotten by travail and pains, and therefore uses all means to obtain that good which faith apprehends in the promise. It seeks glory by grace; it endeavors after communion with God in heaven by working a conformity to God in a believer while he is on earth.

Seals of God

Thirdly, believers are made partakers of the divine nature by the promises as they are the irreversible seals and declarations of God, which He has freely made unto them of His taking them unto Himself in an everlasting communion of life and glory. Heaven is, as Prosper calls it, the only climate where blessedness dwells in its perfection.[6] While we are here below, we are but as kings in the cradle. The throne on which we must sit, the robes with which we must be clothed, the crown that must be set upon our heads, are all reserved for heaven. In this life, there is only a taste of celestial delights and in the other there is a perpetual feast. Here we "see through a glass, darkly; but then face to face" (1 Cor. 13:12). Grace, as Cameron[7] expresses it, connotes a weakness and imperfection[8] and a glory that signifies an abolition and doing away with whatever is weak or imperfect. But all this absolute perfection of happiness which is laid up in heaven for believers is ratified and made sure unto them in the

---

6. *Regio beatitudinus.*

7. John Cameron (1579–1625), Scottish theologian, moderate Calvinist, and professor of theology at Saumur (1618–1620) and Glasgow (1622–1623).

8. *adsignificare infirmatatem.*

promises; and, therefore, they are said to be heirs of the promise (Heb. 6:17). Yea, by the promises they have the pledges and firstfruits of all that happiness which they shall enjoy in heaven given unto them in this life. "Now are we the sons of God," says the apostle, "and it doth not yet appear what we shall be" (1 John 3:2). That is, we now bear His image and likeness, though in a more dark and imperfect character. Our knowledge, our grace, our comforts are all incomplete. "When he shall appear, we shall be like him." That is, when Christ shall come to receive us unto Himself, we shall bear upon us His resemblance in a full and absolute manner, being made one with Him in an everlasting fellowship of bliss and glory. Deservedly, therefore, may the promises that seal heaven to believers in the other life, and begin it in this life, be said to make them partakers of the divine nature.

CHAPTER 5

Promises Are Grounds of Matchless Consolation

Fifthly, the promises of the gospel are truly great and precious in regard of those superlative and matchless consolations which they derive unto believers amidst the changes and vicissitudes[1] that they are subjected unto while they are in the body and bear about them both the remainders of sin and of death. In the sad winter of desertion, when the verdure[2] of all other comforts wither and drop like leaves that are bitten with the frost, the promises are roses that blow in the winter,[3] and do with their beauty delight and [with] their fragrance revive the drooping and dejected soul. "This is my comfort in my affliction," says David, "for thy word hath quickened me" (Ps. 119:50). In the apprehensions of God's displeasure, with which many times the best of saints are afflicted, even to the drying up of all their moisture, they are the only summer snows[4] that cool and allay the scorching heat, and make that Christian that was like a parched wilderness to become like a watered garden.

"As cold waters to a thirsty soul," says Solomon, "so is good news from a far country" (Prov. 25:25). Good tidings from heaven

---

1. *vicissitude*: change.
2. *verdure*: freshness.
3. *rosae in hyeme.*
4. *Aestiva nives.*

by the gospel promises are most welcome in such a condition. In the tempestuous seasons of trouble and affliction, they are sacred and sure anchors[5] to stay and fix believers amidst all tossings, and to make them ride safely without touching upon the sands to be swallowed up in despair or dashing against the rocks to be shipwrecked by presumption. Therefore, the apostle calls them a sure refuge to such as lay hold upon them (Heb. 6:18). In the calm and serene times of peace, they are the only white spread sails,[6] which filled with the sweet breathings of the Spirit triumphantly carry believers on to the fair havens of everlasting happiness. Therefore Paul, within ken[7] of the shore, after the custom of the mariners, gives a joyful and triumphant celeusma,[8] or shout, "O death, where is thy sting? O grave, where is thy victory?" (1 Cor. 15:55). And can all or any of these things be affirmed of the best of earthly comforts? Surely, if we would compare the one with the other, we might quickly find as vast a difference as between a noisome laystall[9] and a precious bed of spices, or between a reviving cordial and a dangerous poison. Forestus,[10] in his treatise *De venenis*, concerning poisons, reports of a woman who had accustomed her body to poisons by making them her usual food, that she had brought herself and her whole constitution to be of the same power as the poison itself was, but yet she retained so much beauty that she allured princes to her embraces, and by that means killed and poisoned them. Not

---

5. *sacrae anchorae.*

6. *vela candida.*

7. *ken*: sight.

8. *celeusma*: a command or call given by the chief oarsman, which gave the time to the rowers.

9. *laystall*: a place where cattle going to market would be held; became a term for a place where dung was accumulated before removal.

10. Petrus Forestus (1591–1597), a Dutch physician commonly referred to as the "Dutch Hippocrates." Forestus had an international reputation and fought against medical quackery.

much unlike this harlot is the world, whose delights and pleasures retain so much of a seeming beauty as to entice many to be enamored with them; but when they are enjoyed by those who eagerly thirst after them, by their deceitful embraces they destroy and kill their lovers. There is a poisonous and contagious breath that comes from them which lays the foundation of a lingering and certain death. And who is there that has inordinately let out his heart unto them that has not experienced the deadly poison which abounds in them? But that we may the better see how far the comforts of the promises excel the comforts of the world, let us weigh them in the balance together and we shall quickly find how greatly they fall short of yielding such real consolations as freely flow from the promises by a due consideration of these four particulars.

The Pure Comforts of the Promises

First, the consolations that are derived from the promises excel in purity the most delightful comforts that are drawn and sucked from the breasts of the world. The promises are the receptacles of the most sincere milk of the Word (1 Peter 2:2);[11] they are bottles filled with the choicest and most refined wines;[12] they are the golden mines that are without dross.[13] The milk, the wine, and the gold that the promises abound with to the nourishing, cheering, and enriching of believers are most pure and free from any alloy that might debase them. The commendations that Plutarch[14] gives of the Spartans, short and weighty speaking, "the Laconic speech has no bark,"[15] is most true of the seven-times tried and refined words of the gospel. They have

---

11. *Mulctralia Evangelica.*
12. *coelestes utres.*
13. *spirituales aurifodinae.*
14. Plutarch (ca. 45–120), Greek Platonist philosopher.
15. Ὁ λόγος Λακόνικος ὀυκ ἔχει φλοιὸν.

neither skin nor husk; they are all pith and substance. But it is far otherwise with the best of earthly comforts which when sublimated and clarified to the very utmost that art and skill can reach are yet accompanied with an inseparable mixture of dregs and lees which minorate[16] their virtue and taint their sweetness. What Crates in Laertius affirms of the pomegranate, "in the fairest pomegranate, there are corrupt and unsavory kernels,"[17] may justly be applied to all sublunary contentment and delights whatever; there are some impurities cleaving unto them by which they glut as well as feed; there is a weft and tang in their farewell that renders them unpleasing as well as a sweetness that makes them desirable.

The Full Comforts of the Promises

Secondly, the comforts of the promises, as they are pure, so are they full and satisfactory, when the best that the world yields serve rather to provoke an appetite than to fill it, to enflame the thirst of desires rather than to quench them, to express an indigence in a restless motion rather than a complacency in a perfect rest. If we could suppose the apple of a man's eye to be as big as the body of the sun, and as piercing as the beams and heat thereof from which nothing is hid, yet among those innumerable objects that such an eye would behold, it could not spy out anything which might be an adequate and proportionate good unto the capacity of the soul. The good that is satisfactory unto it must have two properties; it must be the best and chiefest of goods,[18] that it may fix the appetite,[19] there being nothing desirable beyond it; and it must be the greatest good[20] that it may fill

---

16. *minorate*: diminish or lessen.
17. Ἐν ῥοιᾷ καὶ καλῇ σαωρὸν τίνα κόκκον εἶναι.
18. *bonum optimum.*
19. *sistere appetitum.*
20. *bonum maximum.*

the appetite,[21] and so free it from the vexation of hunger and want. Now the top and cream of all worldly comforts are exceedingly deficient in satisfying the sensitive faculties, and inferior part of the soul, much less can they fill with a grateful satiety and contentment the mind, which is the noble and supreme part of man, and by its creation fitted for communion with an infinite good. When, says Plutarch, did Epicurus[22] cry out "I have fed,"[23] with so much joy and delight, as Archimedes[24] in his mathematical contemplations did [cry out], "I have found"?[25] And when did both they or the whole sect of Epicures and [the] philosophers, in the enjoyment of their sensual and intellectual pleasures, cry out with such strong ravishments of soul they had either fed or found, as a believer does when he has tasted and found the goodness of God in one promise? Listen but a little, and you shall hear in how loud and pathetical a tone David expresses himself when he had but tasted these divine consolations: "Whom have I in heaven but thee? and there is none upon earth that I desire beside thee. My flesh and my heart faileth: but God is the strength of my heart, and my portion for ever" (Ps. 73:25–26). And Bellarmine[26] tells of a pious old man that was wont to rise from prayer with these words always in his mouth, "Be shut, be shut, O mine eyes; for now you shall never see anything more desirable."[27]

---

21. *implere appetitum.*

22. Epicurus (341–270 BC), Greek philosopher and founder of Epicureanism, a school of philosophy centered on "pleasure," or the absence of pain.

23. Βεβρωκα.

24. Archimedes of Syracuse (ca. 287–212 BC), Greek mathematician, physicist, and astronomer. He was one of the leading scientists of antiquity.

25. Ἑυρηκα.

26. Robert Bellarmine (1542–1641), Italian Jesuit, cardinal, theologian, and apologist for the Counter-Reformation of the Roman Catholic Church.

27. *Claudimini oculi mei, claudimini; nihil enim pulchrius jam videbitis.*

The Sure Comforts of the Promises

Thirdly, the comforts of the promises are abiding and sure mercies (Acts 13:34), such which are the crystal streams of a living fountain, and not the impure overflowings of an unruly torrent, which sometimes with its swellings puts the traveler in fear of his life, and at other times shames his expectations of being refreshed by it (Job 6:15). Geographers, in their description of America, report that in Peru there is a river called the Diurnal, or "day-river," because it runs with a great current in the day but is wholly dry at night, which is occasioned, as they say, by the heat of the sun that in the daytime melts the snow that lies on the mountains thereabouts, but when the sun goes down, and the cold night approaches, the snow congeals, which only fed it, and the channel is quite dried up. Not much unlike this river are all worldly contentments, which are only day-comforts but not night-comforts; in the sunshine of peace and prosperity, they flow with some pleasing streams, but in the night season of affliction, they vanish and come to nothing. Then the rich man, as Cyprian says, lies restless upon a bed of down, and fetches deep groans,[28] though he drinks pearls and sapphires.[29] But it is far otherwise with the promises, whose streams of comfort in the time of trouble do usually run most plentifully and refresh most powerfully the weary and afflicted soul to preserve it from dying and fainting away under the pressure of any evil. This was it which made Hezekiah under a sentence of death to revive and to cry out, "O Lord, by these things men live, and in all these things is the life of my spirit" (Isa. 38:16). But if at any time these divine consolations run in a more shallow and spare channel, and vary from their wonted fullness, yet they never prove like waters that fail, or streams that are quite dried up. A believer

---

28. *vigilat in pluma, suspirat licet bibat gemmas.*
29. Cyprian, *Epistle 1. Ad Donatum,* ed. Rigait., p. 6.

may sometime be drawn low, but he can never be drawn dry. While Christ is a full fountain, faith will never be an empty conduit pipe. His comforts may be like the widow's oil in the cruse,[30] where only a little remains (1 Kings 17:12), but never like the water in Hagar's bottle that was quite spent (Gen. 21:15). The widow thought her store of meal and oil to be brought to so low an ebb as that it would serve but for one cake, which two sticks would be fuel enough to bake, and then both she and her son must expect to die, but then the Lord did put forth His power, though not in making the oil and meal to overflow to the feeding of others therewith, but in keeping it from wasting, so as to be a constant supply unto her and the prophet's necessities in the extremity of the famine.

The like apprehensions the dear and beloved ones of God frequently have in their afflictions and temptations which befall them; they think they have scarce faith enough to last one day more, scarce strength enough for one prayer more, scarce courage enough for one conflict more, and then they and their hopes must die and give up the ghost forever. But in the midst of all these fears and misgivings which arise from their hearts, there issues out such a measure of comfort from the promises, which, if it gives not deliverance from their temptations, effects their preservation in them. If it overflows not to make them glad, it fails not to make them patient, and to wait till God send forth judgment unto victory (Matt. 12:20).

The Universal Comforts of the Promises

Fourthly, the comforts of the promises are universal, such as agree with every estate, and suit every malady; they are the strong man's meat, and the sick man's cordial, the condemned sinner's pardon, and the justified person's evidence. But the best

---

30. *cruse*: a jar.

of the world's comforts are only applicable to some particular conditions, and serve as salves for some few sores. Riches are a remedy against the pressing evils of want and poverty, but they cannot purchase ease to the pained. Armor of proof is a defense against the sword and bullet, but can no way serve to keep off the stings of piercing cares; oils and balsams are useful for bruises and broken bones, but they are needless to a hungry man that seeks not after medicines but food. As the hurting power in creatures is stinted and bounded, fire can burn but not drown; water can drown but not wound; serpents and vipers can put forth a poisonous sting but cannot, like beasts of prey, tear and rend in pieces. So, the faculty of doing good, which is in any creature, is confined to a narrow scantling, and reaches no further than the supply of some particular defect. But the comforts and virtue of the promises are in their operations and efficacy of an unlimited extent; they flow immediately from "the Father of mercies, and the God of all comfort" (2 Cor. 1:3), and are, therefore, meet to revive and establish how disconsolate in any kind whatsoever the condition of a believer be. "In the multitude of my thoughts within me thy comforts delight my soul," says holy David (Ps. 94:19). When disquieting thoughts swarmed within his breast, as thick as motes in the sunbeams, and did continually ascend like sparks from a flaming furnace, which the crown upon his head could not charm, which the scepter in his hand could not allay, which the delights and pleasures of his court could not sweeten, then did the comforts of God in His promises, as so many fresh springs in the midst of all his estuations,[31] both glad and calm his unquiet and perplexed spirit. One sun, when overcast with thick clouds which threaten to blot it out of its orb, then enlightens the earth far more than multitudes of stars that shine bright in the clearest night; and so

---

31. *estuations*: disturbances, troubles.

one promise, in armies of changes that befall believers, fills their souls with more serenity and peace than the confluence of all outward contentments can produce under one small and petty cross. A Christian many times walks more cheerfully under sore fiery trials than others in the sunshine of worldly prosperity. The three children walked to and fro with more joy in the furnace than Nebuchadnezzar in his stately palace.

CHAPTER 6

Promises Focus Faith on God in Christ

Having shown what a promise is, and the sundry respects wherein the promises of the gospel are precious by way of eminency and excess, I pass on to the third general head, which is made up of several rules and directions that concern the due application of them, which are by so much the more necessary by how much the promises above all other parts of the sacred oracles of God are most apt to be deeply injured by the two sinful extremes of distrust and presumption. The infirm believer, whose jealousies and misgivings are too strong for his faith, puts away from him the consolations of the promises as small and looks upon them as cordials not strong enough to heal and remove his distempers. The over-secure and self-confident person places his fond presumptions in the room of God's promise and thereby draws as certain a ruin upon himself as he who ventures to go over a deep river without any other bridge than what his shadow makes. I shall, therefore, branch the rules which concern the right use of them into rules positive and cautionary, the one pointing out several duties which everyone must exercise himself in that would willingly reap any real fruit and advantage from the promises, the other forewarning the many errors and mistakes, which are as stones of stumbling to weak Christians, or as stones that lie upon the mouth of the wells of salvation which must be removed before the water of comfort can be drawn from them. I shall begin with the positive rules, which are many.

Eye God in the Promises

First, in the applying of any promise, fix the eye of your faith upon God, and Christ in it. Promises are not the primary object of faith but the secondary; or, they are rather the means by which we believe than the things on which we are to rest. As in the sacraments, the elements of bread and wine serve as outward signs to bring Christ and a believer together, but that which faith closes with and feeds upon is Christ in the ordinance and not the naked elements themselves. So the promises are instrumental in the coming of Christ and the soul together; they are the warrant by which faith is emboldened to come to Him, and to take hold of Him; but the union which faith makes is not between a believer and the promise but between a believer and Christ. And, therefore, those divines who in their catechetical systems have made the formal object of faith to be the promise rather than the person of Christ have failed in their expressions, if not in their intentions, and have spoken rather popularly than accurately. For the object of faith is not an evangelical maxim or proposition,[1] but the person of Christ,[2] as the whole current of Scripture expressions abundantly testify, wherein faith is described by receiving Christ (John 1:12), by believing on Him (John 3:16), by coming to Him (John 6:35–36).

As we cannot come to Christ without the aid of a promise, so may we not rest in the promise without closing with Christ. The promises are but as the field, and Christ is the hidden pearl which is to be sought in them; they are as the golden candlesticks, and He is both as the olive tree which drops fatness into

---

1. *ens complexum.*
2. *ens incomplexum.*

them, and as the light which shines in them; they are as the alabaster box, and He is as the precious spikenard which sends forth the delightful savor; they are as the golden pot, and He is the manna which is treasured and laid up in them; they are as the glass, and He is the beautiful face which is to be seen in them. "We all, with open face beholding as in a glass the glory of the Lord, are changed into the same image from glory to glory" (2 Cor. 3:18).

Directions to Focus Faith

But in looking unto God and Christ in the promise, let the eye of faith be directed especially to these four attributes and perfections of God: the freeness of His grace in making them, the absoluteness of His power to effect them, the unchangeableness of His counsel not to revoke or disannul the least iota of them, [and] the greatness of His wisdom to perform all which He has spoken in the best season and joint of time. These are four such pillars upon which faith may safely lean and which the strength of the most violent temptations can never shake, much less overturn, as Sampson did the pillars of the house against which he leaned (Judg. 16:30).

The Free Grace of the Promiser

First, view with the eye of faith the freeness of God's grace in making so many rich promises. They are all patents of grace, not bills of debt; expressions of love, not rewards of services; gifts, not wages. He that made many out of mercy might without the least umbrage of injustice have made none. Though His truth ties Him to the performance of them, yet His love and mercy only moved Him to the making of them. His promise has made Him a debtor, but free grace made Him a Promiser. And here the assertion of the school may be judged sound: though the will of God be most entirely free in all His manifestations towards the creature, yet upon the voluntary and free precedency of one supposed act we may justly conceive Him to be necessarily obliged to a second.[3] Thus, God was most absolutely free in the making of His promises, but having made them, He is necessitated to the fulfilling of them by His truth. According to that of the apostle, "God, that cannot lie, promised before the world began" (Titus 1:2). And that of the prophet, "Thou wilt perform the truth to Jacob, and the mercy to Abraham" (Mic. 7:20). The making of the promise unto Abraham was free mercy, the fulfilling of it to Jacob was justice and truth.

This direction touching the freeness of God's grace in the promises is exceeding useful to succor and relieve the perplexing fears of the weak and tempted Christian, who, though he has eyes to see the unspeakable worth and excellence of the promises, yet has not the confidence to put forth the hand of faith and to apply them to his necessities. He wants forgiveness of sins but doubts the promise of blotting out iniquities belongs to him. He is naked, and gladly would that Christ might spread the skirt of His righteousness over him to hide his deformities. But alas! What has a leper to do with a royal robe? He is sick and diseased, but the physic that must cure him, the least drop of it is more worth than a world, and he is more vile than the dust. How then can he expect that he should ever be the patient of such a Physician who will be both at the cost to buy the physic and at the pains to administer it? If he had a heart to love God as David, if talents to glorify God as Paul, if he were but an Israelite without guile as Nathanael, then he might have hopes together with them to have his person accepted, his services rewarded, and his imperfections pardoned. But his heart with which he should love God is carnal and not spiritual; his talents

---

3. *divina voluntas licet simpiciter libera sit ad extra, ex suppositione tamen unius actus liberi, potest necessitari ad alteru.*

and abilities with which he should glorify God are few or none; his sincerity which should be the evangelical perfection of all his duties has more than an ordinary tincture of hypocrisy and self-ends mixed with it. With what confidence therefore can such a one draw near to Christ or ever expect to be welcomed by Him?

Now to put to silence these reasonings and to allay these fears that unless checked and bounded oftentimes terminate in the blackness of despair, there is not a more effectual remedy than the consideration of the freeness of the grace of God and Christ in the promises, which are not made to such as deserve mercy but to such as want it, not to righteous persons but to sinners, not to the whole but to the sick. And, therefore, such who through the weakness of faith or the violence of temptations find it difficult to lay hold on the promises of God touching the pardon of sin and the obtaining of life and salvation, let them resolve the promises into the first root and principle from whence they spring, which is not from any good within us but wholly from grace without us; and they will readily find that by eyeing the ground and origin of the promise they will sooner be encouraged and drawn to believe and to lay hold upon it than by looking only to the promise itself. Of all the ways and experiments to bear up a sinking spirit, there is no consideration like this, that from the beginning to the end of our salvation nothing is primarily active but free grace. This is a firm bottom of comfort against the guilt of the most bloody and crimson sins because free grace is not tied to any rules; it may do what it pleases. Somebody who goes to heaven might be the greatest sinner, and what if you are he whom God will make the everlasting monument of the riches of His love and mercy in Christ? This is an impenetrable shield against the constant accusations of Satan drawn from unworthiness, unprofitableness, backwardness to holy duties, and distractions in them. 'Tis true, a believer may say, "I am unworthy, and that which Satan makes the matter of his accusation is the daily matter of my confessions and self-judging before God; the sins which he pleads against me with delight, I bemoan with tears of bitterness. And were the way which leads to heaven a ladder of duties, and not a golden chain of free grace, I could not but fear that the higher I climb the greater would my fall prove to be, every service being like a brittle round that can bear no weight and the whole frame and series of duties at the best far short of the ladder in Jacob's vision, which had its foot standing upon the earth and its top reaching to heaven." But the whole way of salvation from first to last is all of mere grace that the promise might be sure (Rom. 4:16). Every link of the golden chain is made up of free mercy: election is free (Eph. 1:5); vocation [is] free (2 Tim. 1:9); justification [is] free (Rom. 3:24); sanctification [is] free (1 Cor. 6:11); glorification [is] free (Rom. 6:23). And, therefore, though I can challenge nothing of right, yet I may ask everything of mercy, especially being invited by Him who does not feed His people with empty promises but gives liberally unto everyone who asks and does not upbraid, either with former sins or present failings (James 1:5).

The Great Power of the Promiser
Secondly, in the applying of every promise, look with the eye of faith upon the greatness of God's power, which is able to fulfill to the least iota whatever He has spoken, and "to do exceeding abundantly above all that we ask or think" (Eph. 3:20). The confining of God's power according to the narrow apprehensions and dwarfish thoughts that men naturally have of Him in their hearts, the Scripture points out as the chief root of all that unbelief and distrust which is put forth in their lives. Thus, the Israelites in the wilderness were seldom in any exigency which they looked upon beyond the possibility of second causes to deliver them from, but they straightway called also into question the power of God. They spoke against God. They said, "Can

God furnish a table in the wilderness? Behold, he smote the rock, that the waters gushed out, and the streams overflowed; can he give bread also? can he provide flesh for his people?" (Ps. 78:19–20). So, when they were in the long captivity of Babylon, they had many clear and express promises of being restored, and brought back again into their own inheritance; yet measuring the truth of God's Word not by the strength of His power but by the improbabilities and impossibilities which appeared to their reason, they look upon themselves not as prisoners of hope but as free among the dead and as far from any expectation of deliverance as dead and dry bones are from reviving. "Our bones," say they, "are dried, and our hope is lost: we are cut off for our parts" (Ezek. 37:11). Thus, the Sadducees denied and derided the great doctrine of the resurrection as being full of irreconcilable difficulties and inconsistencies. How a body and a soul separated should be reunited; how a body not only separated from the soul but dissolved into dust should be recompacted; how dust scattered and blown up and down should be re-collected; [all these were] altogether beyond the line of their reason to fathom or compass. Our Savior, therefore, points out the ground of their error to arise, not only from their ignorance of the Scripture which had foretold it, but also of the power of God which was able to effect it: "Ye do err, not knowing the scriptures, nor the power of God" (Matt. 22:29). Necessary, therefore, it is in the making use of any promise that a believer has such conceptions of the power of God as that whatever lets[4] and impediments arise between the promise and the fulfilling of it, though as high as mountains and as strong as the gates of hell be, yet by faith looked upon as difficulties which cannot check the power of God but only magnify it; for else, if once we come to have jealous thoughts of the divine arm in which we trust, or to fear

---

4. *lets:* hindrance.

that it might be encountered by some insuperable opposition, the hopes and expectations that we have of any good from the promise must needs be weak and uncertain.

When God had promised to make Abraham the father of a seed as numerous as the stars of heaven or the dust of the earth, though reason could not but suggest unto him how unlikely he was to be a father and Sarah to be a mother, when age had dried up his body and deaded the womb of Sarah, yet says the apostle, "Against hope believed in hope, that he might become the father of many nations" (Rom. 4:18). That is, when nature afforded no ground of hope or encouragement to confirm his expectation in the fulfilling of the promise but suggested many posing arguments to implead and gainsay the truth of it, and to make his faith as feeble as his body, yet then he exercised the fullness of assurance in believing and of hope in expecting the accomplishment of all that God had spoken. He staggered not at the promise of God through unbelief, but was strong in faith, giving glory to God, being fully persuaded that what He had promised He was able also to perform (vv. 21–22). So when afterwards God called him to that signal trial of his faith and obedience in the offering up of his only son, and appointed himself to be the priest as well as Isaac to be the sacrifice; and though the stroke which Abraham's hand was stretched forth to give would not only have ended the life of his son, but have cut off also the promise at the very root because in Isaac his seed was to be called, yet by the same eye of faith by which before he looked through a dead womb, he now looks through a bleeding sword unto the power of God, accounting that He "was able to raise him up, even from the dead" (Heb. 11:19). That is, he believed that rather than the promise of God should not be certain, the resurrection of Isaac should be more miraculous than his birth; and that God would magnify His power in raising him out of the ashes of a consumed sacrifice to be the heir of the promise rather than let one tittle of His Word fall to the ground unfulfilled. And thus should every believer as a true child of Abraham endeavor to do in looking from themselves unto the power of God for the making good of any promise which they in prayer do earnestly seek in faith do really believe, [and] in hope do patiently wait for and expect. And though difficulties and temptations should arise, which their reason cannot answer, [and] their strength cannot repel, yet not to cast away their confidence but to cast themselves upon Him who is both the strength and wisdom of His people, with whom things that are utterly impossible with men are not only possible but easy for Him to bring to pass and to effect. Oh, the happy peace and serenity that a believer enjoys in every estate and condition which befalls him, that can thus rest and stay himself upon the promise and power of God! No valley of trouble will be to him without a door of hope, no barren wildernesses without manna, no dry rock without water, no dungeon without light, no fiery trial without comfort, because he has the same Word and the same God to trust unto whose power opened the sea as a door to be a passage from Egypt to Canaan, who fed Israel in the desert with bread from heaven, and water from the rock, who filled Peter's prison with a shining light, who made the three children to walk to and fro amidst the fiery furnace with joy and safety.

The Unchangeableness of the Promiser

Thirdly, to sweeten the application of every promise, exercise your thoughts and faith on the unchangeableness of the purpose and counsel of God to fulfill whatever His promises declare. The promises of men, though they be the expressions of an intended and resolved good unto that person to whom they are made, yet they are subject to a deficiency from a double principle. Sometimes, through a want of power to give a being and existence unto what they have spoken, they prove rather the fruitless wishes of a friend that means well than the performances of one that has ability to turn his words into deeds. But that which most frequently makes the promises of men to be as abortive conceptions, and not as full births, is the mutability and inconstancy of their wills, whereby they are not only apt to recall and suspend the fulfilling of what they promised, but also to change their love into hatred, and their promises into menaces. The tree that in the summer is much esteemed and sat by for the grateful shade which it affords, in the cold winter is often cut down for fuel; and so the same person, which in the heat of affection is made the object of many favors, in the keen blasts of jealousy becomes the subject of revenge and ruin. But it is far otherwise with the promises of God, whose power no lets or impediments can arise to hinder, whose will no contingencies or emergencies can fall out to alter. All His promises are in Christ not yea and nay, but in Him, "Yea, and in him Amen" (2 Cor. 1:20). "He is not a man, that he should repent" (1 Sam. 15:29). He is the Lord that changes not (Mal. 3:6). [He is] the Father of lights, with whom there is no variableness or shadow of change (James 1:17). And that the heirs of promise might yet be more abundantly confirmed in the immutability of God's counsel, He has added to His Word His oath, wherein He pawns[5] His being, life, righteousness, truth, mercy, [and] power to perform all that He has spoken so "that by two immutable things, in which it was impossible for God to lie, we might have a strong consolation" (Heb. 6:18). This consideration, therefore, of looking unto the unchangeableness of God in the constant use and application of His promises, as it serves to point out the wide difference between the promises of God and the promises of men, the one being as frail and uncertain as bubbles, no sooner made than broken, like breath on steel, as soon off as on; the other like firm

---

5. *pawns*: held as a pledge.

rocks of adamant, which can neither be broken or moved. So, also, is it exceeding useful to preserve and keep believers from being injurious to their own comforts, or God's honour, who, from the frequent changes which they find in themselves, are apt to apprehend the like to be in God. They recede from God, and then complain that God departs and withdraws His presence from them, not unlike those who, in a constant motion upon the waters, move from the land and then fancy the land and trees to move from them when God still retains the steadfastness of His purpose and will, without any variation or difference by all the mutations that are in the creature.

The failings in our vows, the unevenness in our duties, the waverings in our faith, produce no alterations in Him who is "the same yesterday, and to day, and for ever" (Heb. 13:8). "If we," says the apostle, "believe not, yet he abideth faithful: he cannot deny himself" (2 Tim. 2:13). This was all holy David's salvation and desire, all that his heart had to build upon and to satisfy itself with, that though his house was not so with God, that is, did fail much of that exactness and purity that therein God required, which he had solemnly vowed, and therefore did justly deserve to be cast off, yet God had made with him an everlasting covenant, ordered in all things and sure (2 Sam. 23:5). Oh! How sad would the condition of every believer prove if the cornerstone of their salvation should be laid upon no other foundation than their own frail and mutable wills; if as often as they are wanting to themselves, God should be wanting to them; if as often as they provoke His justice, He should presently revoke His mercy; if as often as they break their vows with God, He should cancel His covenant with them. But forever blessed be the God and Father of mercies who has not made our life to be in our own keeping, nor founded the bottom of our happiness and comfort upon my strength, ability, freedom, or inherent grace already received, which we are apt to waste and to betray into the hands of every temptation. But [He] has wholly fixed it upon an irreversible covenant of grace transacted between Him and Christ, upon promises of mercy ratified and confirmed to us by the broad seal of heaven and the oath of God, unto which we may daily fly for refuge as the only sanctuary when pursued with the guilt of any sin, upon which we may lay hold with both hands, as upon a sure anchor, when assaulted and buffeted with the fury of Satan's temptations.

The Wisdom of the Promiser

Fourthly, in making use of the promises, direct the eye of your faith to the wisdom of God, by which the various blessings that are held forth in them are dispensed and given to believers in the fittest and best season and thereby become both the more remarkable and the more useful. The works of God's providence have a beauty and luster set upon them from the appointed time and season that He has allotted unto them; the light of the day becomes more desirable by the interposition of the night; the rest and darkness of the night is rendered more grateful by the labors and toils of the day. The former and the latter rain, He gives in season (Jer. 5:24), the one to bring forth and cherish the new sown seed, the other to ripen and make fruitful the harvest. The summer and winter by an inviolable ordinance, He has made to succeed each other, the one to be as a key to open the womb of the earth that it might discharge itself of its many births; the other as a key to shut it so that it might not languish and grow barren by an unintermitted travel. Now, if the wisdom of God has to these common mercies, wherein His enemies have a share (as well as others), set such appointed times, as may make them more useful and beneficial to His creatures, certainly He will not fail to perform to His people the promises of His free grace in that season and fullness of time that may best suit their welfare and His glory. Promises are not made and fulfilled at the same time any more than sowing and reaping are on the same day. God has in His Word recorded them as so many discoveries of His immutable counsel and purpose that thereby faith might have a sure ground to rely upon Him in all exigencies, and to expect a relief from Him; but the season and time of performance God has reserved to Himself as best knowing not only what to give but when to give. So that believers, though they may plead to God His promise, must yet be careful not to confine and limit Him to times that they judge fittest; but they ought wholly to resign themselves to His wise dispose, to whom every creature looks and receives their meat in due season (Ps. 145:15). If He feeds the ravens when they cry, much more will He satisfy His children when they pray; if to the one He opens His hand and gives liberally, to the other He will open His pity and give above what they can ask or think [Eph. 3:20].

This consideration of the wisdom of God in the timing of His promises to the fittest season is exceedingly useful to correct the hasty and impetuous desires of many Christians, who, if their mouths are not filled as soon as they are opened, if God's promises are not fulfilled as soon as they be pleaded, if they do not have when they ask, they straightaway, like Rachel, cry out that they die, or, like Jonah, say that it is better for them to die than to live (Jonah 4:3), because they do not obtain, not what God's will [is], but what their own will suggests to be best. Watches that go fastest do not always go truest; no more are desires that are most hasty most regular. It is good in prayer to have the desires winged with affection and to be like an arrow drawn with full strength; but yet there must be a submission exercised unto the holy and wise will of God that so it may appear that we seek Him in a way of begging, and not by way of contest; that we do not make Him the object only of our duties and ourselves the end, but Him to be both the object and the end of every service that we give to Him.

CHAPTER 7

Conditions, Interdependence, Frequency, and Persistence

The first direction has much exceeded the bounds which at first were allotted unto it in my thoughts, who did not intend to make so great a disparity between it and the ensuing directions, as to make the one to have the dimensions of a large building and the rest to be after the model of a small cottage. I shall, therefore, so far censure it myself as to acknowledge that more has been done than the laws of a just symmetry and proportion can either defend or excuse and so leave it.

Promises Are Conditional in Performance

The second direction is that though the promises be absolutely free in the making of them, having no other cause than God's will, no other motive than His love and mercy, yet in their performance they are conditional and have a dependency upon duties in us. They are fulfilled not only in us but by us. To a clear explication of this rule, I shall propound an ordinary but yet a necessary distinction concerning the promises, which is this: there are promises of grace, and there are promises which are made to grace. The one are so absolute as that they do not depend upon any grace in us foregoing, or suppose any good qualifications in us to be partakers of them; such are the promises of conversion and regeneration in which grace makes way for itself and works all the initial preparations without any concurrence or activity on our part, we being as fully passive in our second birth as we are in our first birth, in our regeneration as in our generation. The other promises made to grace are conditional, not as supposing anything to be performed by our strength and power, or as if the conditions were causes meriting the grace promised; but they are conditional in regard of a precedent qualification and fitness in the subject that is to partake of them, without which they cannot be fulfilled, grace being made the condition of grace. Thus, pardon of sin is promised to him that repents, justification to them that believe, glory to him that is sanctified, a crown to him that perseveres, and increase in grace to him that improves grace received. But the absolute promise of conversion, and giving of spiritual life, though it has a kind of opposition unto conditional promises in not requiring that aptitude and qualification of the subject by grace for the fulfilling of it, as the others do for the performance of them; yet is it not absolute in opposition to the use of external means, which God has appointed as a necessary way to obtain converting grace. For as the decrees of God, though peremptory and unchangeable, do not exclude the endeavors of the creature and the working of second causes, no more does the absoluteness of God's promise in conversion shut out but rather include the use and exercise of all means that lead to the end. True it is that to hear savingly, to mingle faith with the Word, men cannot by any natural power or ability in the least measure do; but yet God has commanded that they should attend upon the ordinances and afford their presence to hear the Word when preached and delivered unto them. And though these be such actions which have no immediate influence to the begetting or working of grace, yet are they so far necessary, as that no man can promise unto himself that ever he shall be converted who either neglects or refuses the using of those means in which God is pleased to dispense His free and undeserved grace.

Silencing the Negligent

This direction is very useful in a double respect, to which it fitly serves, first, to silence the profane cavils of those who make no other use of their natural impotency to good and of the power of God in conversion than to exempt themselves from all attendance upon ordinances, God being able by a powerful voice to bid them arise from the dead, when, like Lazarus, they lie in the grave of their sins, as well as heal them; when, like the cripple, they lie at the pool of the sanctuary, expecting the moving of the Spirit upon the waters, no impediment being able to cross or frustrate the purpose of the Almighty. But as in other works of God, so in conversion, not His power only, but His will which is commensurable to His power and modifies it in the working is to be observed and heeded. Some things He effects without means, not because His power is infinite and stands not in need of any other assistance, but because His will is [that] it should so work. Other things, though as immediately wrought by Himself, are accomplished in the use of means, not that either His will or power are unable to give an existence unto them without any secondary helps, but that His pleasure is to have them so wrought and perfected. Such is the work of making a new heart, of infusing spiritual life where it is wanting, which though it be wholly and only from God Himself, is yet ordered by Him to be effected in the use of means. As physicians put their physic in certain syrups and liquors, which are not at all of themselves operative but serviceable to the medicine that works the cure,[1] so does God by His ordinances which are channels and conduit-pipes[2] designed for grace to run in, convey and dispense

---

1. *vehicula medicina.*
2. *canales gratiae.*

the precious blessing of a new and spiritual life to those upon whom He is pleased to bestow it. And, therefore, as the plea of those is both weak and impious who contemptuously turn their backs upon the preaching of the Word, and other external helps, as needless and unnecessary to conversion, it being God's sole work, so their expectation in the close will be both sad and fruitless, ending rather in a just turning into hell by God than in a saving and effectual turning through grace unto God.

Encouraging the Diligent

Secondly, it serves to excite and quicken believers to an unwearied diligence in holy duties, as being the ready and expedite way to obtain their desires in the fulfilling of any promise which they stand in need of. The penny was given to the laborer in the vineyard not to the loiterer in the marketplace (Matt. 20). And the reward in the promise is not to him that sits still and expects salvation to drop into his lap, but to him that seeks and pursues after it, making God's promise not a ground for his idleness but a spur and motive to his diligence. The promises are wells of salvation flowing with the waters of life, but yet the strong Christian that expects to be refreshed by them must be at pains to draw water out of them (Isa. 12:3). They are full breasts of consolation; but yet the weak Christian, who is as the newborn babe, or new-yeaned[3] lamb, must suck these breasts (Isa. 66:11), if he will be satisfied with their aliment. "Though you be weak and little," says Augustine, "yet seek and exact with importunity mercy from God. Do you not see how the young lambs do with their heads force down the milk from their dam[4] that they may be filled therewith?"[5] To wrestle and strive with God like Jacob

---

3. *new-yearned*: newly born.

4. *dam*: mother.

5. *Etsi infirmus, etsi parvulus exige a Deo misericordiam. Non vides perbreves agnos, capitibus pulsantes ubera matrum, ut lacte satientur?*

for the gaining of a blessing is not superfluous because God has promised it, but [it is] necessary because He has commanded it: "I will yet for this be enquired of by the house of Israel, to do it for them" (Ezek. 36:37). So, Jeremiah 29:11–12, "I know the thoughts that I think toward you…thoughts of peace, and not of evil.…Then shall ye call upon me, and ye shall go and pray unto me, and I will hearken unto you." Calling on God is not for His information but for the exercise of [a] believer's obedience and submission. He will have faith as a hand to work, as well as a hand to receive. It was a scandal that Pharaoh brought upon the religion of the Israelites that it made them idle (Ex. 5:8). And it is a wrong done to the promises of the gospel by carnal libertines, who make use only of them to countenance their sloth and not to quicken their obedience. None that ever I have heard of have held marriage vain or unnecessary for the propagation of mankind, who have yet been of [the] opinion that the soul is not generated but immediately created and infused by God; no more can any man rationally conclude that because the promises of God are the declarations of His unchangeable purpose and will, therefore, duties and endeavors are superfluous to the effecting of any good which He has promised to confer upon us.

The Dependency of One Promise on Another, Which Must Not Be Broken, Nor Inverted

The third rule or direction is that there is a sacred concatenation[6] and dependency of one promise to another, which may not be violated, and a fixed order which may not be inverted.

The Sacred Bond

First, the mutual tie that is between the promises in the application of them must not be broken. As the duties of the law are

---

6. *concatenation*: a series of interconnected things.

copulative, and may not in the obedience that is yielded unto it be disjoined (James 2:20), so are the blessings of the promises, which may not be made use of as severed from each other, like loose and unstringed pearls but as collected and made into one entire chain. God has linked the promises of pardon and repentance together, and no man may presume that God will ever hearken unto him who begs the one and neglects to seek the other. When He pacifies the conscience, He melts the heart, and works repentance, as well as seals forgiveness. So, likewise, has God inseparably knit grace and glory together as that none can lay a just claim to the one who is not first made partaker of the other; no man can expect to be an heir of heaven that is not first a saint on earth. Holiness leads to happiness, as the rivulet to the sea, as the way to the end; the one is as the foot of the ladder and the other as the top. "Glory, which is the highest round, is not attained by flying but by an orderly ascending unto it," says Bernard;[7] the intermediate steps must not be skipped but trodden. Oh! how vain then are those men's hopes, and how sinful are their practices, who stand upon the battlements of hell and sport themselves with all the sensual delights of the flesh, trampling under their impure feet with scorn the precious promises of holiness by which they should be moulded unto all obedience! And yet at the same time stretch forth a hand of presumption to lay hold on the promises of life and eternal glory, as if they were the true heirs and proprietaries thereof. But their forlorn condition, which they would not see by the light of the Word, they shall read by the flames of hell, being infinitely more pressed down under the weight of God's displeasure and endless despair than ever they were lifted up with the transient hopes of happiness by a carnal and ungrounded presumption.

---

7. *Summitas scalae attingitur, non volando, sed ascendendo.*

The Sacred Order

Secondly, in the applying of the promises, the order and method of them is not to be inverted but to be observed. The promises which God has made are a full storehouse of all kinds of blessings; they include in them both the upper and the nether springs, the mercies of this life and of that which is to come. There is no good that can present itself as an object to our desires or thoughts of which the promises are not a ground for faith to believe and hope to expect the enjoyment of. But yet our use and application of them must be regular, and such as suits both the pattern and precept which Christ has given us. The pattern we have in that most absolute prayer of His (Matt. 6:9–10), wherein He shows what is chiefly to be desired by us: the sanctification of His name in our hearts, the coming of His kingdom into our souls, the doing of His will in our lives are to be sought for before and above our daily bread. We may not be more anxious for food than for grace. The precept we have in His most heavenly sermon, "Seek ye first the kingdom of God, and his righteousness; and all these things shall be added unto you" (Matt. 6:33). Promises are to be improved in prayer and other duties primarily for holiness and secondarily for other outward comforts. The soul is more worth than body, as the body is more worth than the raiment, and, therefore, the principal care of every one ought to be to secure the welfare of his soul by interesting himself in the promises of life and eternal happiness. But yet even here also a method must be observed and the law of the Scripture must be exactly followed, which tells us that God first gives grace and then glory (Ps. 84:11). As it is a sin to divide grace from glory, and to seek the one without the other, so is it also a sin to be preposterous in our seeking, to look first after happiness, and then after holiness. No man can rightly be solicitous about the crown, but he must first be careful about the race; nor can any be truly thoughtful about his interest in the promises of glory that does not first make good his title to the promises of grace. Salvation, endless life, fellowship with angels, and the firstborn of heaven, they are, as Augustine calls them, the last things[8] in order that God has to give, or that we have to ask; and, therefore, we may not anticipate the order of them but wait upon God in His own way. What the apostle says concerning the resurrection, that in Christ all shall be made alive (1 Cor. 15:22–23), but every man in his own order, may be truly spoken concerning the promises of the gospel, that in Christ all shall be fulfilled, but every promise in its own order.

Meditate Seriously, Frequently on the Promises

The fourth direction is to meditate thoroughly and frequently upon the promises, and to deal with them as the Virgin Mary did with the things that were spoken concerning Christ: she "kept all these things, and pondered them in her heart" (Luke 2:19). The limbeck[9] does not put any virtue into the herbs, but it distills and extracts whatever is efficacious and useful from them. The bee does not derive any sweetness to the flower, but by its industry it sucks the latent honey from it; so meditation conveys nothing of worth unto the promise, but it draws forth the sweetness and discovers the beauty of it, which else without it would be little tasted or discerned. I have sometimes thought that a believer's looking upon a promise is not unlike a man's beholding of the heavens in a still and serene evening, who, when he first casts up his eye, sees haply a star or two only to peep, and with difficulty to put forth a feeble and disappearing light; by and by he looks up again and then both their number and luster are increased; a while after, he views the heavens again, and then the whole firmament, from every quarter, with a numberless multitude of

---

8. *promissum finale.*
9. *limbeck*: an apparatus used for distilling.

stars, is richly enameled as with so many golden studs. So, when a Christian first turns his thoughts towards the promises, the appearances of light and comfort which shine from them do ofttimes seem to be as weak and imperfect rays which neither scatter fears nor darkness; when again he sets himself to ripen and improve his thoughts upon them, then the evidence and comfort which they yield to the soul is both more clear and distinct. But when the heart and affections are fully fixed in the meditation of a promise, oh!, what a bright mirror is the promise then to the eye of faith? What legions of beauties do then appear from every part of it, which both ravish and fill the soul of a believer with delight? How does he sometimes admire free grace whereby God becomes a debtor, not by taking anything from us but by promising great things unto us? How does he triumph in the fullness of mercy which overflows in it as being enough to fill the widest capacity and to supply the greatest necessity? How does he stay himself upon the stability of the promise, it being founded upon strength itself, the Strength of Israel, who cannot lie? One promise thoroughly ruminated and meditated upon is like to a morsel of meat well-chewed and digested, which distributes more nourishment and strength to the body than great quantities taken down whole. Samson when he had made a great slaughter of his enemies, and laid them heaps upon heaps, yet he complains that though God had given him so mighty a deliverance, he was ready to die for thirst (Judg. 15:18). So, many Christians who make it their work to heap promise upon promise may yet be sorely distressed for want of comfort, if, by meditation, they do not dive into the depths of the promise. The water wherewith Samson was refreshed came forth out of a hollow place which the Lord clave in the jaw; and the springs of comfort which believers drink of come out of the cliffs of the promise, which faith and meditation makes in it. Let me, therefore, persuade such as are desirous and willing to make the utmost of every promise to put in practice this much neglected duty, without which every ordinance is of little fruit. The Word as it must have preparation before it, which like the plough fits the ground for the reception of the seed, so must it have meditation to follow after, which is as the harrow to cover and hide the new-sown seed, or else the fowls of the air will pick it up. The sacrament, as it is food to be received with an appetite, so is it to be digested with meditation, else the nourishment will be little. The promises, as they must be read in the Scripture with diligence, so must they be called to remembrance by many serious musings and actings of our thoughts upon them, else they will never prove strengthening and reviving cordials. Roses are sweeter in the still than on the stalk; and promises are more fragrant in the heart than in the book. The grapes hanging on the vine do not make the wine that cheers the heart of man but the grapes that are squeezed and trodden in the winepress. No more do the promises as they stand in the Bible work joy and gladness but as they are pondered in the mind, and, like pressed grapes, have their juice and virtue drawn from them, which by a percolation in the thoughts turns into a most sovereign and precious liquor.

Be Much in the Application of the Promises

The fifth direction is to be much in the use and application of promises, though we do not find such visible effects either of grace or comfort issuing from them as we expect or desire. Elijah, when he went up to the top of Mount Carmel and fell upon his face before the Lord to pray for rain, he sent his servant seven times to look towards the sea before he saw so much as the appearance of a cloud of a handbreadth, yet was he not discouraged (1 Kings 18:43). So believers, though they have been much in musing upon the promises in their thoughts, frequent in pleading and spreading them before the Lord in prayer, and after all their looking towards heaven say as the servant of Elijah when he looked towards the sea, there is nothing;[10] yet must they not cast away their confidence in them or neglect the daily use of them, because the promise and the word that goes forth out of God's mouth shall not return unto Him void but shall accomplish that which He pleases, and it shall prosper in the thing whereunto He sent it (Isa. 55:11). The manner of the fulfilling of it may be various, but the performance of it is most certain. The blessing of the promise descends, sometimes, like rain in visible showers, producing the sensible effects of joy and peace in the soul; sometimes, it falls like dew in a silent and imperceptible way, without making any discernable alteration in the heart of a believer; the virtue which it puts forth is real but yet withal hidden and secret. As gold put and boiled in broth helps to make it strengthening and cordial, which if weighed afterwards in the scale is found to lose little or nothing of its former weight, or to suffer any diminution of its substance, so the promise when much meditated on, when frequently applied by a believer to his present straits, yields a secret influence and support, though to his apprehension no virtue or quickening appears to have issued from it. Then, it is as the cork to the net to keep it floating in a sea of difficulties, when every moment we look for nothing else but a dismal and irrecoverable perishing amidst those many rolling waves and billows that pass over us.

This direction I propound the rather because that Christians lying under fears, darkness, and temptations are not seldom like hasty patients under diseases and infirmities, who, if they find not a present benefit in the use of physic, either in the removal or in the abatement of their distempers, straightways conclude that it were better for them to bear the pain of the disease than to trouble themselves with the daily applications of fruitless remedies and prescripts, not considering that physic may be useful to

---

10. *non est quicquam.*

prevent the danger of the disease when it does not work the cure to keep them from growing worse, though it do not make them better. So believers, when, by the use of promises and other ordinances, they find no sensible alteration for the better in respect of their present condition are apt to throw off the use of means as things that stand them in little or no stead. Though they use the precepts of the Word as a lamp to guide their feet, yet they stumble; though they use the promises as a staff to support them, yet they fall; though they beg and pray for strength, yet they are feeble; to what end, therefore, should they be much in the use of such helps, as they cannot find either to relieve them or better them? Such expostulations and complaints I shall only answer with a suitable story related in the lives of the ancient fathers, which is this: One of the fraternity came to the old father and complained, "Father, I do often desire of the ancient fathers some instructions for the good of my soul, and whatsoever they tell me, I forget all." The old man had two empty vessels, and bid him bring the one and pour water into it and wash it clean, and then pour out the water and set it up clean in its place. Which, when the young man had accordingly done, he demanded, "Which now of the two vessels is the more clean?" The young man answered, "That into which I poured water, and washed it." Then replied the old father, "So is the soul which oftentimes hears God's Word, though it remember not what it has heard; yet it is more cleansed from sin than that soul that never comes to hear." And so may I say to them that complain they ruminate often upon the promises in their thoughts, plead them in their prayers, read them in the Word, but yet find no benefit or fruit from them: that in so doing they are not only more holy and free from lusts than others who neglect them but far better than otherwise themselves would be should they not be employed in such spiritual and blessed services.

CHAPTER 8

Waiting, Sorting, Selecting, Depending, and Gratitude

Continue in a Holy Waiting upon God

The sixth rule or direction is to abide and continue in a holy waiting upon God until He who is the Maker of the promises becomes the fulfiller of them. "Our eyes wait upon the LORD our God," says the psalmist, "until that he have mercy upon us" (Ps. 123:2). Some promises are like unto the almond tree which puts out upon the first approach of the spring and brings forth an early fruit; they are not long pleaded ere they be fulfilled and have their blessings like ripe fruit to drop into the mouth of the eater. Others are like to the mulberry tree, which is slow and backward in the imparting of its sap unto the branches; they are long before they bud forth into any appearances which may discover any step and progress to be made in order to their future accomplishment. So that they who are the inheritors of them, though they need not to fear their failing the appointed time, yet they need patience to expect and wait their fulfilling. The great promise which God made to Abraham of multiplying his seed like the stars of heaven (Gen. 15:5) did for 215 years continue its motion like to a slow-paced planet, having in all that tract of time gone little of that course which it was to finish, for Abraham was seventy-five years old when the promise was made and 100 years old when Isaac, who was the first blossom of that promise, was born. Isaac was threescore years old before Jacob was born; Jacob was 130 years old when he went into Egypt, and then there were no more than seventy souls that had issued from the loins of Abraham. But yet in the latter 215 years, "When the time of the promise drew nigh, which God had sworn to Abraham, the people grew and multiplied in Egypt" (Acts 7:17). They that were but seventy at their going into Egypt were at their coming forth 603,550, the males only being numbered from twenty years old and upward, besides the tribe of Levi, which was forbidden to be counted (Num. 1:46–47). Seeing, therefore, that there is ofttimes a long interval between the seedtime and the harvest of the promise, between its making and its fulfilling, it is necessary for believers to wait upon God, who is one that can best date and time His own promises[1] and to expect with patience the appointed time of the promise, which at the end shall speak and not lie. "Though it tarry, wait for it" (Hab. 2:3).

Now, if you ask what waiting is, it is not any particular grace, as varnish is not a particular color, but it is the companion well-nigh of all graces, and, therefore, in Scripture, we shall find it to be joined to the chief of graces, so as by its conjunction with them to add a perfection and luster to them. It is joined with faith, "He that believeth shall not make haste" (Isa. 28:16). With hope, "It is good that a man should both hope and quietly wait for the salvation of the LORD" (Lam. 3:26). With patience, "The husbandman waiteth for the precious fruit of the earth, and hath long patience for it" (James 5:7). With submission and content-ment, "Rest in the LORD,[2] and wait patiently for him" (Ps. 37:7). With perseverance, "Keep mercy and judgment, and wait on thy God continually" (Hos. 12:6). All these graces thus coupled with waiting is a believer to exercise in his pleading before God the

---

1. *optimus opportunitatis arbiter.*
2. Spurstowe adds: "[or wait silently for the LORD]".

performance of any promise, and to take heed that he let not his faith to end in diffidence, his hope to languish into despair, his submission and patience to turn into murmurings, his perseverance to expire in backsliding, and to say as that wicked king, "This evil is of the LORD; what should I wait for the LORD any longer?" (2 Kings 6:33). A good heart, though it will not let God wait long, no not at all for its obedience, yet it will wait as long as God sees good for His promise, saying only with David, "Remember the word unto thy servant, upon which thou hast caused me to hope" (Ps. 119:49).

Make Choice of Some Special Promises to Resort to in Extremity

The seventh direction is to single and cull out of the many promises which God has made for pardon, holiness, protection, provision, some one or two of every kind, which we may resort unto with speed in any extremity. Weak and infirm persons, besides the many physical herbs, distilled waters, magisterial powders, costly electuaries with which their closets are plentifully furnished, have usually some peculiar cordial which in the day they carry about them and at night set at their bed's head to prevent and repel fainting fits. So should believers, besides those promises of all sorts with which they are to store themselves, have in a constant readiness some few special promises, which upon every occasion that may befall them, they may quickly have recourse unto, both for support and comfort. And here, though I shall not prescribe and limit any in their choice but leave them to the free use of such Scriptures and promises as themselves by experience have found to be full of life and sweetness, yet it will not be amiss to recommend the use of some few eminent promises of divers kinds out of the full storehouse of the Word, which may serve as so many meet cordials to revive the spirit of drooping Christians amidst the several kinds of necessities that may afflict them.

Burdened with Guilt

Are any burdened with the guilt of sin, so as that their soul draws nigh unto the pit of despair? What more joyful tidings can ever their ears hear than a proclamation of free mercy made by the Lord Himself unto believing and repenting sinners? What more glorious and blessed sight can their eyes ever behold than the name of God written in sundry of His choice attributes, as in so many golden letters for them to read? "The LORD, The LORD God, merciful and gracious, longsuffering, and abundant in goodness and truth, keeping mercy for thousands, forgiving iniquity and transgression and sin" (Ex. 34:6–7).

- He is the Lord, who only has the absolute power of life and death[3] in His hands; but

- He is the Lord God merciful, who far more willingly scatters His pardons in forgiving than executes His justice in condemning, like the bee that gathers honey with delight but stings not once unless she be much provoked.

- He is gracious, not incited to mercy by deserts in the object but moved by goodness in Himself. His love springs not from delight in our beauty but from pity to our deformity.

- He is longsuffering, bearing with patience renewed and often repeated injuries, which He might by power revenge upon Him who is the doer.

- He is abundant in goodness; grace overflows more in Him than sin can do in any. Sin in the creature is but a vicious quality, but goodness in Him is His nature.

______

3. *jus vitae et necis.*

- He is abundant in truth; as He is good in making the promises, so is He true in performing them; when men deal unfaithfully with Him, He breaks not His covenant with them.

- He keeps mercy for thousands. Former ages have not exhausted the treasures of His mercy so as that succeeding generations can find none. There are still fresh reserves of mercy, and that not for a few but for thousands.

- He forgives iniquity, transgression and sin; not pence but talents are forgiven by Him; not sins of the least size are only pardoned but sins of the greatest dimensions.

And as this promise in which the name of God is so richly described fully answers the hesitancies, doubts, and perplexities of such who fear their iniquities for number to be so many, for aggravation to be so great, as that sometimes they question, "Can God pardon?" [and] sometimes, "Will He ever show mercy to such a wretched prodigal?" So, likewise, may that blessed promise made unto believers (Hos. 14:5–7) exceedingly support such who mourn under their want of holiness and complain of the weakness of their grace, fearing that the little which they have attained unto goes rather backwards than forwards. God Himself having promised that He will be as a dew unto them, which shall make them to put forth in all kinds of growth: "[They] shall grow as the lilly, and cast forth [their] roots as Lebanon. [Their] branches shall spread, and [their] beauty shall be as the olive tree…they shall revive as the corn, and grow as the vine."

What more comprehensive summary can there be either of God's goodness or of a believer's desires than there is in this one promise? Wherein He has promised to make them grow in beauty like the lilly, in stability like the cedar, in usefulness like the olive, whose fruit serves both for light and nourishment, in spreading like the vine and in their increase like the corn, God Himself being both the planter and waterer of all their graces.

Full of Fears

To them who are full of fears through the approach of dangers which they have no hope to avoid or power to overcome. How full of encouragement and comfort is that promise of protection and safety? "When thou passest through the waters, I will be with thee; and through the rivers, they shall not overflow thee: when thou walkest through the fire, thou shalt not be burned; neither shall the flame kindle upon thee" (Isa. 43:2). Water and fire are two evils in which none can be with their nearest friends without perishing with them. Who can save a Jonah when cast into a boisterous sea but God? And who can walk in the fiery furnace with the three children and not be consumed but the Son of God? In the prison, one friend may be with another, in banishment he may accompany him; in the battle, he may stand by him and assist him, but in the swelling waters and in the devouring flames, none can be a relief to any but God; and He has promised to believers to be with them in the midst of both [of] these, that so in the greatest extremities which can befall them, they may fully rest assured that nothing can separate God from them, but that He will either give them deliverance from troubles, or support them under troubles: "He did not take the martyrs out of the flames, but did He forsake them in the flames?"[4]

In Bad Condition

Lastly, to them, the meanness of whose condition may seem to expose them above others to hunger, cold, nakedness, evils that make life itself far more bitter than death, how full of divine sweetness is that blessed promise of provision? "The young lions

---

4. *Martyres non ripuit, sed nunquid descruit?*

do lack, and suffer hunger: but they that seek the LORD shall not want any good thing" (Ps. 34:10). The Septuagint renders it "the great wealthy men"[5] of the earth, who, like beasts of prey, live upon spoil and rapine, who think that in the hardest times that can come they shall be eaten up last; they shall be bitten with hunger and perish by famine when they who fear the Lord shall be in want of nothing. The widow's little barrel of meal in the famine yielded a better supply than Ahab's storehouse and granary, her cruse had oil in it when his olive yards had none. Oh! how securely and contentedly then may a believer who acts his faith in such promises lay himself down in the bosom of the Almighty in the worst of all his extremities! Not much unlike the infant that sleeps in the arms of his tender mother with the breast in his mouth, from which as soon as ever it wakes, it draws a fresh supply that satisfies its hunger and prevents its unquietness.

Consider of the Examples to Whom Promises Have Been Fulfilled

The eighth direction is in the making use of any promise to parallel our condition with such examples which may be unto us as so many clear instances of the goodness and faithfulness of God in His giving unto others the same or the like mercies which we seek and beg for ourselves. As the promises are useful to strengthen faith, so are examples to confirm and assure sense, which is continually apt to implead what faith believes and to question what God has spoken. God has promised that "though your sins be as scarlet, they shall be as white as snow; though they be red like crimson, they shall be as[6] wool" (Isa. 1:18). But sense suggests, "What possibility is there that ever such a change

---

5. πλούσιοι.

6. Spurstowe adds, "as white as."

should be? Can soap, nitre,[7] [and] water make scarlet to be as white as undipped wool?" No more can it be that the ingrained spots and stains of sins so often reiterated, so long persisted in, should be done away and the sinner be clothed with the white robe of innocency. God says, "I will heal backsliding, I will love them freely" (Hos. 14:4). He will love freely without respect of persons; He will pardon freely without respect of sins. But sense that shuts the door of hope, which He has opened, sometimes calls in question His power, "Can He work wonders among the dead? Can He raise from the rottenness of the grave such as have lain long putrefying in it?" Sometimes, [it] disputes His mercy, "Will He ever remember the chief of sinners? Will He be gracious to the rebellious that have both neglected and refused the tenders of salvation which have been often made?" Now, when a believer beholds the pregnant examples both of His power and love set forth in the Scriptures in His converting a stubborn Manasseh; in His translating into paradise a bloody robber; He in His casting forth of devils out of Mary Magdalene, a notorious harlot; in His changing Paul a persecutor into an apostle; in His compassionating[8] and healing Peter that sealed his backsliding with a curse; in His bringing salvation to Zacchaeus, a hateful extortioner; then the expostulations of sense and carnal reasonings are put to silence; then he concludes with confidence that the promises are a sanctuary for the penitent and lifts up his feet with cheerfulness to run unto them; then he pleads the bounty and faithfulness of God in the performance of His promises unto others as a strong argument to show the like mercy unto him. Thus David, in his low condition, strengthens his faith and hope in God from this ground, "Our Fathers trusted in thee... and were not confounded" (Ps. 22:4–5).

---

7. *Nitre*: a cleaning agent.

8. *compassionating*: showing mercy or compassion to.

This direction is always of use to believers in the ordinary and daily application which they make of the promises, because examples, as they are powerful in persuading obedience to every precept which commands it, so are they also efficacious to strengthen and confirm faith when exercised on any promise. But it is chiefly useful in extremities when dangers which are insuperable do at any time environ us. Besides the promises which faith uses as a support, it is good to have in our eye some such example as Daniel, whom God preserved in the lions' den, sealing up their mouths by His power that they should not hurt him, before the king had sealed the mouth of the den with his signet, that he might not come forth. When sad desertions and temptations afflict us, it is useful to call to our remembrance some such instance as Heman who complains that he was laid in the lowest pit, that he was afflicted with all [of] God's waves, that he was ready to die from his youth up, [and] that he was distracted while he suffered his terrors (Ps. 88). And yet afterwards he becomes "the king's seer in the words of God, to lift up the horn" (1 Chron. 25:5). That is, he, as a prophet, is especially employed to set forth the mighty acts of God's power in psalms and songs of praise and thanksgiving. When sore afflictions are multiplied upon us, which for their weight are more heavy than lead, for their bitterness more bitter than gall and wormwood, it is good to have in our thoughts some such example as Job, that we be not wearied and faint in our minds. "Take, my brethren, the prophets, who have spoken in the name of the Lord, for an example of suffering affliction, and of patience," says the apostle (James 5:10). What a map and spectacle of misery is Job made above others? How various and how great were the afflictions with which he was exercised? Sabeans [and] Chaldeans destroy his substance; fire from heaven consumes his servants; a great wind smites the four corners of the house, and destroys all his children; ulcers [and] boils break forth upon his body; keen and unjust censures from his friends vex his soul, and yet the happy close and end that the Lord makes with him are as famous as his miseries were. His riches and substance are doubled, his number in children equalled, his body healed, and his name cleared by God Himself. These and such like instances when suited with a believer's condition contribute much to the suppressing and keeping of that despondency and dejection of mind, which the extremity of trials in any kind is apt to subject the best of Christians unto, and cause them to renew their confidence in the promises, and in hope to expect the performance of them, because that others in the same or not unlike case with themselves have found the faithfulness and goodness of God in His supporting them under their burdens, and giving perfect deliverance from them according to His promise.

Preserve Communion with the Holy Spirit Entire

The ninth rule or direction is to keep and preserve entire our communion with the Holy Spirit. The dependency which every believer has on the Spirit is very great, he being unto the soul as the soul is unto the body, the original and principle of all spiritual life and motion. What are any until He quicken them, and by His power fashion them unto holiness, but as so many lifeless lumps of undigested clay? And what are the best without His continual breathings upon them, but as so many disjointed and weak members, which have neither constancy nor uniformity in their motions or actions? Grace in its vigor and strength abides in the heart, as light in the house, by way of emanation and effusion, rather than by inherency. An instrument, when it has an edge set upon it, does not at all cut anything, till it be guided and moved by the hand of an artificer; no more does a Christian, when he has a habitual aptitude through grace to work, yet do or perform any service without the concurrence and assistance of the Spirit of Christ, quickening, exciting and applying the habitual power unto particular duties. Necessary, therefore, it is that believers be circumspect in maintaining their communion with Him, and not to provoke Him to stand at a distance from them, who is the fountain both of their grace and comfort. But the necessity of it will more particularly appear if we consider in how much need we daily stand of the constant assistance and powerful operations of the Holy Spirit to make the applications of all the promises to be effectual unto us both for support and comfort. He alone it is who is the mighty worker of that noble and divine grace of saving faith, by which believers are enabled to lay hold of the promises, and by them of Christ, in whom they all meet, as so many lines in their common center. He it is, who opens the eyes of the understanding, and fills the heart with a heavenly light, by which the worth and preciousness of those things which are given of God in the promises are judged and discerned. He it is, who brings to our remembrance the faithful sayings of the gospel, and makes them to be as words spoken in season to him that is weary. He it is, who teaches believers to plead the promises in their supplications unto God, and when they know not what to pray for as they ought, makes request for them with groanings that cannot be uttered [Rom. 8:26]. He it is, who by way of obsignation[9] seals and ratifies the promises unto the faithful, and that in a peculiar and transcendent manner. In the assurance and security which is given for outward things, we only have the wax sealed with the impression and sculpture of the seal, the signet sealing is not at all looked after; if the one be safe, it matters not though the other be lost. But in the confirmation of the promises, believers possess both. They have the Holy Spirit, who is as the Seal sealing, and the graces of the Spirit, which are as the seal sealed and printed upon their hearts. The Spirit by His special testimony assures them of the

---

9. *obsignation*: confirmation.

certainty of their salvation, and seals them up unto it, according to that of Paul, "The Spirit itself beareth witness with our spirit, that we are the children of God…and joint-heirs with Christ" (Rom. 8:16–17). The graces of the Spirit, which are His lively image and impress upon their souls, also evidence and confirm the same thing, according to that of the apostle, hereby "we know that we have passed from death unto life, because we love the brethren" (1 John 3:14).

It is, therefore, a direction of great importance unto all who would gladly reap profit and advantage from the promises to keep firm and to strengthen their communion with the Spirit, who is the only Counselor to instruct them how to manage the promises to the best improvement of them, the most powerful Advocate to furnish them with arguments to plead at the throne of grace their right unto them and their interest in them, the most effectual Comforter to support their hearts with confidence to fill them with joy while they wait upon God for the performance of His promises unto them. If He be grieved by our careless demeanor towards Him, it is not any promise that can make us glad; if he be provoked to withdraw and suspend His light, there are no irradiations from the promises that can free us from the darkness of desertion; if He be made to turn our enemy by voluntary defections from Him, none of the promises can speak peace unto us. How vain and ungrounded then are the presumptions of those who build their hopes of heaven and salvation upon the promises of mercy, and yet neglect all communion with the Spirit of holiness, [or those] who rest in the testimony of their own spirit, misguided by false rules, and cheated by Satan's subtleties, and look not at all after the testimony and witness of the Spirit, without whom all the promises of the gospel are but as deeds and instruments with labels hanging at them without seals to confirm them, which do not operate or convey anything of right unto those that are possessed of them?

Be Truly Thankful for the Least Dawnings of Mercy

The tenth direction in the right use of the promises, no less weighty than any, is to be truly thankful for the least dawnings of mercy for the smallest pledge and earnest of comfort which the promises at any time do afford unto us. The angel rebuked and reproached those "who hath despised the day of small things" (Zech. 4:10), who with mournful eyes, with unbelieving and misgiving hearts, did look upon the poor and mean beginnings of the rebuilding of the Temple, as such which were altogether unlikely to terminate in a glorious structure, and to have the top-stone thereof laid with shoutings and acclamations of joy. And no less are those Christians to be reproved who esteem any of the consolations of God to be small; who, if they be not at first filled with the spiritual suavities of the promises, take little or no notice of the support and sustentation which they receive daily from them; who, if they presently enjoy not what they hastily desire, can neither thankfully accept of any pledges of mercy which God has freely vouchsafed them, nor patiently wait for the sure performance of the promises which He has made them. It is the usual method of God to fulfill His promises by certain steps and degrees, to make His salvation to break forth like the morning which begins in an imperfect twilight but ceases not till it grow up into a bright day. The first glimmerings of peace and comfort which spring from the promises are accompanied with great mixtures of darkness, but yet they are of a growing and prevailing nature, and, therefore, are not to be despised but to be thankfully acknowledged and rejoiced in as the happy earnests of an ensuing day in which the soul is as full of spiritual serenity and joy as the firmament is of light when the sun is in its vertical point. In the bestowing of His favors, God deals with believers as Boaz did with Ruth. He first gave her a liberty to glean in his fields, then invited her to eat bread at his table and to dip her morsel in the vinegar, and lastly gave himself. So God, first, in a sparing manner, and at some distance, makes a discovery of His love and good will unto them, then, in a more familiar and friendly way, He encourages them by His promises to draw near unto Him and to taste how good the Lord is to those that fear Him. And then as the complement of all, He gives His Spirit into their bosoms to assure them of His love, and their interest in whatever might make them perfectly happy. "After that ye believed, ye were sealed with the holy Spirit of promise," says the apostle (Eph. 1:13). But the ready and speedy way to obtain all this is to be truly thankful for the least appearance of mercy that shines forth from the promises, and to count it worthy of all acceptation to receive it with such joy as the morning was wont to be anciently saluted, when the people went out and cried, "Welcome, such light."[10] To such, God speaks as our Savior did to Nathanael, "Because I said unto thee, I saw thee under the fig tree, believest thou? thou shalt see greater things than these" (John 1:50). Are you thankful for a spark, for a beam of light? You shall be satisfied and filled with the Fountain of light itself. Do you bless God for crumbs that fall from His table? You shall be feasted with the marrow and fat things of life and salvation. "The ungrateful person receives no increase but what he has formerly received turns to his ruin. But the grateful person is always thought worthy of more ample rewards," says Bernard.[11]

This direction I gladly would that those Christians should often have in their thoughts who are so much in complaining what they want, as that they never bless God for what they enjoy. When any come into their company, their ears are continually afflicted with their mournful notes. How few their comforts are, how little the benefit is [that] which they reap by the promises,

---

10. χαῖρε φῶς.

11. *Ingrato nihil augetur, sed quod acceperat vertitur ei in perniciem. Fidelis autem in modico, censetur dignus munere ampliori.*

but their hearts are never quickened to bless God on their behalf, by their thankful acknowledgment of the least mercy that God has vouchsafed them when as indeed it is a temper most befitting a Christian not to let the smallest of His favors to pass unobserved or unacknowledged. The swine eats the fruit that falls from the tree but never looks up from whence it comes. But the dove picks not up a grain without casting up its eye to heaven; it eats and then looks up, then picks again, and then looks up again. And so should a believer lift up an eye of thankfulness unto God for every beam of light and hope which he beholds in His Word, though it shine only through a narrow cranny. "I thank God in Christ," says holy Baines,[12] "sustentation I have, but spiritual suavities I taste none." When we do not lie rejoicing in the arms and bosom of God as a Father, it is a mercy worthy of our thankfulness that we may lodge safely in His house; when we do not behold the smiles of His face, it is a mercy that we may hear His voice in His Word; when we have not the ring put on as an ornament, it is a favor that we have any piece of a broken ring left with us as a pledge and token that in our extremity He will not forsake us.

To increase the number of these positive rules were a task not in itself difficult, nor yet happily to many weak ones altogether unnecessary, but because it is far easier for a physician to write recipes than for a patient to take the many repeated and continued potions, I shall forbear to add more, as fearing I have been already too burdensome and prolix[13] in these, and shall only recommend what has been spoken to the serious practice of believers without the least infringing of their liberty to use others which either their own or others, experience may

---

12. Paul Baynes (ca. 1573–1617), Elizabethan Puritan, successor of William Perkins at St. Andrew's Church in Cambridge, and author of a celebrated commentary on the first two chapters of Colossians.

13. *prolix*: of long duration, lengthy.

suggest as profitable. And so I pass on to the second sort of rules which are cautionary, the end of which chiefly serves to discover sundry errors and mistakes, which in the application and use of the promises are as dangerous to believers as unseen rocks and unfounded shallows are to mariners, and, therefore, are to be carefully heeded and to be avoided by them.

CHAPTER 9

Mere Assent and Understanding Humility

Rest Not in a General Faith

The first cautionary rule is to take heed of resting in a general faith, which goes no further than to give a naked assent unto the promises of the gospel as true but does not put forth itself to receive and embrace them as good. True faith is not an act of the understanding only but a work of the heart also, "With the heart man believeth unto righteousness" (Rom. 10:10). As it yields an assent unto the truth of the promise, so it exercises fiducial application of it unto itself and thereby drawing near unto Christ wholly throws and casts itself upon Him for life and happiness, not at all looking after any other help. Maldonate[1] is pleased to make himself and his reader merry with that usual distinction of our divines, by which faith is distinguished into a historical, miraculous, temporary, and saving faith, and, playing upon the word *fides*, says that the Protestants have "as many faiths as there be strings upon a fiddle."[2] But it is not his scoff and sarcasm that can elude either the truth or the necessity of the distinction; when as the Scripture tells us of many that

---

1. Juan de Maldonado (1533–1583), Spanish Catholic biblical scholar, who was highly critical of the Reformation, but whose commentaries on the Bible were influential.

2. *Tot fides quot in lyra.*

believed, and yet did never embrace Christ with their hearts as their only Savior, or confidently rely upon the promises of His mercy. Simon Magus is said to be a believer (Acts 8:13). And yet Saint Peter tells him that he is in the gall of bitterness and the bond of iniquity (v. 23). The multitude believe in Christ's name, but yet He would not commit Himself unto them, for He knew what was in man (John 2:25). He did not own them as those to whom He would impart the saving mysteries of His gospel, or join Himself unto them in the same bond of love and friendship, as He did with those who with an entire and sincere heart believed on Him. The five foolish virgins went far in their waiting for the bridegroom; they took lamps with them to meet Him, and kept their lights for a season burning; but yet at His coming, the door was shut against them (Matt. 25:11–12). And shall the faith of God's elect and sanctified ones be of no better alloy than the faith of hypocrites and other wicked and impenitent sinners? Yea, shall the confession of Peter concerning Christ, "Thou art the Christ, the Son of the living God" (Matt. 16:16) be no whit better than that of the devils, who, with a loud voice, cry out, "Jesus, thou Son of God" (Matt. 8:29)? Shall it be distinguished from it no more in its worth than it is in its words? But as the palest gold much exceeds the most glittering alchemy, which though it seem to outvie[3] the gold in its luster, yet has it not the least affinity with it in its real virtue and worth; so the smallest grain of saving faith, by which a believer closes with Christ in the promises, is more precious and excellent than a mere assent unto the truth of the Word, which rests in the understanding but has no quickening influence upon the will and desires, the one being only a bare credence and the other a divine affiance. This was it which put a wide difference between Peter's confession of Christ, and the devil's acknowledgment of Him, as Augustine

---

3. *outvie*: outdo.

well observes, "This spake Peter, that he might embrace Christ; this said the devils, that Christ might depart from them."[4] And this fiducial application is the distinguishing character which the Scripture makes between the faith of true believers and others, it being sometimes described by a rolling and staying of itself upon God (Isa. 50:10), sometimes by a trusting in Him (Isa. 26:4), sometimes by receiving of Christ (Col. 2:6), sometimes by a coming unto Him (John 6:35–36). All which expressions do speak the spiritual motions and affections of the heart towards Christ in cleaving and adhering unto Him, which believers only exercise and not hypocrites or castaways. And, therefore, they are said not to rely on God, or to look towards Him (Isa. 31:1); not to trust in Him (Ps. 78:22); not to receive Christ (John 1:11); not to come unto Him (John 5:40). Their faith is a form of faith, but it wants the power and efficacy which accompanies saving faith.

This cautionary rule is with the more circumspection to be heeded in regard that multitude of professors rest themselves contented in that general acknowledgment and assent which they yield to the truths of the gospel, though haply the chief inducement by which they are led unto it be no other than custom, education, or the authority of the church. They think that believing there is a God, that Christ is the Savior of the world, that He died for sinners, is faith enough to carry them out of the wilderness into Canaan, out of the world into heaven. But alas! this and much more may be believed, and yet no benefit at all accrue unto them who are persuaded of the certainty of these supernatural verities. Here, the logicians rule holds true: physic is not given to man's nature to cure the species,[5] but [it is given] to every man to heal his person.[6] Christ and His promises are

---

4. *Hoc dicebat Petrus, ut Christum fide amplecteretur; hoc dicebant Daemones, ut Christus ab eis recederet.*

5. *Medicina curat Socratem, non hominem.*

6. *in individuo.*

not beneficial unto any but unto them who make a particular application of both unto themselves. What comfort is it to an insolvent debtor to believe that there are rich mines of gold in that land into which he is fled to shelter himself from his creditors? What relief is it to a thirsty man that there is a full vintage of cordial and refreshing wines growing not far from him if he has no hope that he shall taste the least drop of it? What satisfaction is it to a condemned person to be assured that there is a pardon granted and sealed for many if there be no ground for him to conceive that his name is included in it? No more can it advantage any man to believe that Christ died to reconcile sinners to God, and that by a glorious resurrection from the grave He has ascended the throne of majesty, and lives forever to make intercession for them, unless with the belief of these blessed truths there be conjoined a particular reliance upon Christ for salvation, and a casting of a man's self into the arms of His free mercy for the obtaining of the forgiveness of sins and the justifying of His person at the tribunal of God. Do not the devils believe [in] God and tremble (James 2:19)? Do they not acknowledge Christ His Son (Luke 4:34)? And bow the knee unto Him (Phil. 2:10)? Do not they know and believe that Christ died in general for sinners and that they which fix their confidence in Him shall be saved by Him? What article of the creed is it which they yield not an assent unto? And shall the faith whereby believers are justified not exceed the faith of these infernal spirits?

Assent of Devils and Christians
But if it be said that the assent which the devils yield is full of force and coaction and is commanded by the evidence and majesty of those infallible truths which they do not at all love or affect but the general belief which Christians have of the revealed truths of the gospel is altogether free and voluntary and

is thereby distinguished from the faith of devils. This difference, though it may seem at first blush somewhat specious, yet is it both insufficient and impertinent for that end to which it is assigned; in regard that the distinction which it makes of the one assent from the other is from what is merely accidental, and not from what is essential to the nature and being of faith. For they who make faith to be an act of the understanding only and to consist in an assent unto the truth of those things which God has revealed cannot properly fetch the essential difference which is between the faith of devils and the faith of Christians, from the voluntariness or involuntariness of the assent, from the liking or disliking of the truths which they believe because those are acts of another faculty in which by them faith is not acknowledged to be seated. Besides the assent which the good angels give unto the glorious truths of the gospel, which with diligence they look into (1 Peter 1:12), is both voluntary and delightful, and yet it is most distinct and differing from the credence and assent which believers give unto the same truths, it not being accompanied with a particular application and reliance for life and salvation as it always is in believers who do, with a justifying faith, embrace and apply the promises of the gospel unto themselves. A man may be called to be a witness to a will to aver[7] the truth of it, though he have no legacy given unto him in it; so the angels, as so many heavenly witnesses, affirm and assent unto the truth of those things which Christ has declared in His gospel, as in His last will and testament. But believers are as so many legatees,[8] which have particular blessings therein bequeathed unto them, and, therefore, must not rest in a general belief of the truth of the things but must claim their propriety and interest in them before they can ever have any benefit or comfort from them.

---

7. *aver*: assert the truth of.

8. *legatee*: a person to whom a legacy is bequeathed.

General Faith Commended

But if it be further objected that the Scripture in many places attributes salvation to a general faith, and that the centurion's faith, which our Savior so much commended (Matt. 8:10), seems to imply no more than a historical belief of Christ's power and divinity, that Peter's confession of Christ (Matt. 16:16) was but general, that Martha's faith (John 11:27) was of the same stamp, that Saint John's character of the new birth is set forth by a general faith, "Whosoever believeth that Jesus is the Christ is born of God" (1 John 5:1). To the solving of this doubt a double answer may be given.

1. That in those times, the difficulty lay rather upon the assent than upon the affiance, and the question then was more about the person of Christ than the office of Christ. Now, because it was a great matter in the first dawnings of the gospel to believe Him to be the Messiah, whose outward appearance was so mean and contemptible to the eye of the world, therefore, the Scripture much magnifies and heightens this act.

2. Though the Scripture expressions lay much upon this one act of faith, yet they do not exclude but suppose the other acts of faith to be joined with it. To a true believing, there are three acts necessary: knowledge, assent, fiduciary application. But yet the Scripture oftentimes describes faith by one of these acts, "This is life eternal, that they might know thee the only true God, and Jesus Christ, whom thou hast sent" (John 17:3). In knowledge, there are couched and included the other two acts of faith in which the powerful reception and embracing of Christ for salvation chiefly consists. So when it is set forth by an assent unto the truths of the gospel, there is implied not only a bare persuasion of the mind but an affectionate cleaving and adherence of the heart unto the promises of God made in Christ, by which the soul of a believer is fortified against despair, which the historical belief of them does not in the least measure expel or

overcome. And, therefore, though the papists deride this special apprehension and application of Christ as a mere conceit and unwarranted fancy; though formal professors carelessly neglect it, and take all to be well enough with them as long as they do not question what the Scripture reveals, yet must not any that look after the real enjoyment of comfort and peace from the promises please themselves in a general assent, which is little worth, but must endeavor to clear and evidence their peculiar interest in Christ and His promises by a fiducial application of them unto themselves.

Pore Not on the Measure of Humiliation

The second cautionary rule is to take heed of poring too much upon the measure and degrees of humiliation, as if there were any certain and regular standard by which all humiliation must be measured before ever we may justly claim an interest in the promises, or so much as put forth a hand to touch the hem of Christ's garment that our bloody issues may be healed. True it is that the invitation which Christ makes (Matt. 11:28) is only to them that labor and are heavy-laden to come unto Him that He may give them rest, because they do best taste the sweetness and prize the happy enjoyment of a heavenly rest and peace. But yet all whom Christ invites to come to Him are not alike burdened with the weight and pressure of their sins, or do equally labor under the sense of God's wrath and displeasure. Some are not only heavy-laden with their sins but have their bones broken with the weight of them so as that they roar by reason of the continual disquietness of their heart. Others, though they walk mournfully under their sins, yet are not bowed down under so great a weight, nor express themselves in such loud and passionate complaints. True it is that Christ as a Physician goes only to the sick and not to the whole (Luke 5:31). But yet all are not afflicted with the same violence, though all be sick of the same disease. Some are so affected as that for a season they seem to lie under the calenture[9] and rage of despair itself. Others, again, are sick of their sins after a more mild and gentle manner. Like to an overcharged stomach, they loathe what before they loved; the iniquities that before they swallowed down with delight they vomit up in their confession to God and acknowledge them to be full of nothing but bitterness. But yet wearisome nights through the grinding pains of a guilty and stung conscience are not appointed unto them; they lie down upon the bed of sorrow but not upon the rack of horror. Now the ground of this wide difference that is between the children of God in their first conversion and turning unto Himself chiefly arises from the wisdom of God, and the liberty which He is pleased to take unto Himself in the effecting of His counsels and purposes. For God, being a most voluntary agent, does not tie Himself to a like certain and unaltered constancy in the time, measure, and proportion of His working upon His children; but being free and wise, without limit, and above measure, much diversifies sometimes the duration and continuance of their humiliation and sorrow by making the darkness in some to be shorter, and in others to be longer. Sometimes, He differences the measure, making the pangs and throws of the new birth to be in some both few and easy; in others, to be many and full of extremity. Sometimes, He alters the most usual manner of His working in proportioning sin and sorrow to each other, and does not make the terrors and affrightments[10] for sin to be parallel to the heinousness of the rebellions that have been persisted in against Himself. Paul, a persecutor, is from heaven smitten with trembling and astonishment so as that for three days he sees neither the light of the sun, nor tastes ought of any food (Acts 9:9). But Zacchaeus, a publican and

---

9. *calenture*: delirium caused by sunstroke.
10. *affrightment*: the state of being frightened.

extortioner, is not stricken from the tree upon which he climbs to behold Christ by any rays of majesty and dread shining from His face upon him. But [he] is like ripe fruit gathered by the hand, not shaken off by a tempestuous wind. By a soft and mild voice that may allure and not affright, he is called to come down to entertain Him who brought salvation unto his house (Luke 19:5). But yet both these, though by much differing means, are effectually brought home to Christ and made partakers of life and happiness by Him.

This cautionary direction is given not as an encouragement to any to slight the necessity of humiliation, as if they might without all remorse and brokenness of heart for their sins interest themselves in Christ and His precious promises, and in one moment leap out of the dregs and lees of their natural corruption (on which they have been long settled) into an estate of purity and blessedness, but it is chiefly for these three ends.

To Direct

First, to direct such as mourn under the sense of their sins that are of a deep and double die to look more to the quality of their humiliation than to the quantity, and to try it rather by the touchstone than to weigh it by the balance, because it is not the measure but the truth of it that makes it saving. The mariner in a calm may sometimes apprehend as certain ruin to befall him as in a storm; and so a sinner may see himself in a lost and forlorn condition out of Christ, though he be not broken with the fierce tempest of God's displeasure but by more gentle yet powerful convictions of the Spirit made apprehensive of the absolute necessity of a Savior to free him from the maledictions of the law, and to restore him to an estate of happiness. Humiliation, as it is God's work, so the measure of it is of His ordering and appointing, and in it deals as a wise Physician, who does not give the like doses or quantity of physic to every patient;

but what may best fit the strength and constitution of him that is to receive it, or like the prudent husbandman whom God has instructed to discretion who does not use the same threshing instrument to beat out the more tender grain which he does to the hard. The cartwheel is not "turned about upon the cummin; but the fitches are beaten out with a staff, and the cummin with a rod" (Isa. 28:27).

To Inform

Secondly, to acquaint such whose former wickedness of life has been full of notoriety in many reiterated backslidings from God and rebellions against Him; and yet have passed through the pangs of the new birth without those extremities that usually are measured forth to great sinners, to walk humbly with their God, and to make up what has been wanting in the intension of their sorrow in the extension and continuance of it, often bringing to remembrance the foulness of those iniquities which might have made far greater rents, and more ghastly wounds in their consciences than ever they sustained had not God varied His wonted way and method in which He walks towards refractory and obstinate sinners, making their agony and pains to be proportionable to the heinousness of their pollutions. They which pay small fines do commonly sit at the greater rent. And those Christians who obtain their peace and reconciliation with God upon more easy and cheap terms than others do and must expect that it will cost them more to preserve it and to keep it from suspicions and doubts about the truth of it than usually it does those the foundations of whose peace have been laid in a thorough and most deep work of humiliation.

To Relieve

Thirdly, to antidote and relieve weak and tempted Christians against their own fears and Satan's wily suggestions, which are oftentimes mingled with those complaints, which they pour forth concerning their un-meetness to take hold of the promises of mercy and to apply the salvation of Christ unto themselves. Gladly, they would that their souls might be refreshed with the least drop of the comforts of the promises, with which others are filled, that they might but touch the garment of Christ into whose sides and wounds others do put their hands, crying out with confidence, "My Lord, and my God!" But alas! they dare not do it. What is in others a duty would be in them a presumption for to do. What others are invited to do, they apprehend they are commanded to forbear; in [this] regard, they have not yet undergone such shakings and batterings by the law, as they have heard, read, and known to be in others far less sinners than themselves. Now, the ground of such fears and misgivings, as keep off the soul from closing with Christ and His promises, chiefly arises from their heeding more the measure of their humiliation than the truth of it, and the ascribing of the saving property in it, rather to the quantity than to the quality. But all humiliation for sin is then saving when true; and then true when it drives a sinner utterly out of himself, and stirs up a vehement thirsting after Christ, and a settled resolution to cleave wholly to Him as his Lord and Savior; [and] as his King, to exercise His just sovereignty over him; as his Priest, to mediate unto God for him. And for all other steps or degrees of humiliation, which troubled souls too often look upon as necessary and due qualifications to fit them for their drawing near unto and embracing of Christ and His promises, expecting after such a number of throws, such a measure, height, and continuance of sorrow to find themselves nearer unto Him than before. They are herein, methinks, not much unlike those foolish children, who, being deceived with the seeming sloping of the heavens, do strongly fancy that if they were but on the top of such an hill, or such a tree, then they might play with the sun, put out the stars with their sticks, and discover what kind of man he is that dwells in the moon. But when they have thoroughly tired themselves in running thither, they find the heavens to be at as great a distance from them, and as far out of their reach as at first. So, after all their most bitter lamentations for sin, they will at length find that a precise adequation[11] between sin and sorrow can never be attained unto, it being absolutely impossible sufficiently to mourn for any one sin according to its just merit. "You may sooner," says Bernard, out of Ambrose, "find those who have kept their innocency unspotted than you can find any that have bemoaned their sins with a meet repentance."[12]

---

11. *adequation*: being made commensurate.

12. *Facilius invenies eos qui innocentiam servaverunt, quam qui congruam egerunt poenitentiam.*

CHAPTER 10

Providence, Curiosities, and Carnal Reasoning

Eye Not Providences More than Promises

The third cautionary direction is to take heed of observing and eyeing the providences of God above His promises so as to build the foundation of our confidence upon them when successful, or when cross and unpleasing to weaken the expectation of faith in the fulfilling of any good which the promise as a ground of hope holds forth unto us.

Providence Is Not the Ground of Faith

First, believers are to be cautious of making the most successful providences the ground of their faith or hope, without looking unto the promises which are the only firm pillar upon which every believer may safely found his prayers in the seeking, and his confidence in the obtaining, of any good that he asks at God's hands. This caution is the more necessary in regard that in these times multitudes of professors highly magnify the providence of God and use it as the only argument to persuade both themselves and others, that their ways and persons are both most pleasing unto God, who, by a succession of many wonderful providences, effects their undertakings for them in the midst of many intervening difficulties. But they seldom or never make any mention of the promises, either as the light by which their ways are directed, or as the spring from whence their encouragements and comforts flow and arise. Yea, oftentimes when they are at a loss in the Word, and cannot find the least footstep in it which may allow or justify the paths they walk in, they then shelter themselves under the covert of providential successes, as that which gives a fair testimony unto the goodness and justice of their ways. But as the providences of God are not to be neglected or undervalued by Christians, being full of deep and unsearchable wisdom, so are they warily to be used as a single light and evidence for the putting of men upon great undertakings, or to be the only cynosure[1] for their direction and guidance in them. The starlight of one single promise is of more use to Christians than a constellation of many providences both to assure them in their ways and to support them under any difficulties that they may meet with, as may appear in these three particulars.

1. The light and evidence which arises from the promise is far more clear than the light of providence, and, therefore, more meet both to direct and comfort believers that look unto it and seek an establishment of their ways from it. The promise is written in fair and capital letters, which those that are of the lowest rank in knowledge and wisdom may easily read and discern. It makes wise the simple, and being pure, enlightens the eyes (Ps. 19:7–8). But the providences of God are written in dark and illegible characters, which, though they may soon be discerned to be His hand, yet to decipher the sense and meaning of them is a task that ofttimes exceeds the line of human wisdom. They are like the handwriting upon the wall (Dan. 5:5), where part of the hand that wrote it, Belshazzar saw, but the meaning of it neither he nor the most learned of his Chaldeans could find out. To interpret the mind of God in His providences requires the

---

1. *cynosure*: something that serves for direction or guidance.

skill and wisdom of a Daniel who was filled with an excellent spirit of knowledge and understanding. But to know His will in His promise it is enough if a man be a Nathanael, an Israelite in whom there is no guile; the path of them is plain and "wayfaring men, though fools, shall not err therein" (Isa. 35:8). Providences God uses as His ciphers many times to hide His secret and His counsels from the eyes of men; but the promises are always as His letters of love, in which He reveals Himself unto believers and acquaints them both of His peculiar love and care to them, and of their duty and obligation unto Himself.

2. The promises exceed in certainty the most constant dispensations of providence. The tenure by which any blessings are given, and to which we are entitled only by providence, is not so firm and sure, as that which is derived unto us by the promise. By the one we are made no better than tenants at will and at the discretion of their Lord, who, though He let them enjoy rich possessions and revenues, may yet at His own pleasure remove them and take all into His own hands; by the other, we are made heirs of all the good things that are given unto us, and so may plead the promise of God as our right, they being a part of that portion which He as a Father is pleased to bestow upon us for our more comfortable subsistence in our present pilgrimage. Oh! how slippery, then, is the foundation of those men's comforts, which is only built upon the dispensations of providence, and not upon the stability of the promise? How unsound are their evidences which altogether stand in the success of their achievements, and in the prosperity that has followed them in all their paths, which may in one moment be turned into a sad change, having the same hand of providence which was wide opened in its bounty to them, lifted up in its displeasure against them.

3. The promise exceeds providence in the purity and sweetness that it derives and conveys to every external mercy, which without it are not freed from that vexation and vanity which sin

has subjected every creature unto. Providence dispenses blessings, but the promise only sanctifies them. The one gives the possession of them, and the other the true fruition of them. This is that which makes a wide difference between the temporal mercies which believers enjoy, and those which wicked men ofttimes partake of in greater abundance from the hand of God; "A little that a righteous man hath is better than the riches of many wicked" (Ps. 37:16). His dry morsels are sweeter than their dainties; his small pittance is more satisfactory than their plenty. For the wicked have all these outward and inferior things only from the mere general bounty[2] of God, which does not remove the encumbrances, the vacuity and vexation that are entailed upon them by sin. But the righteous has the same things given unto him by the right of a promise,[3] which sanctifies the gifts of common providence, and takes away from the creature that curse wherein it was wrapped through the sin of the first Adam.

While, therefore, men please themselves in the single interest and right of providence to their earthly comforts, and look not unto the conveyance of them by the promise, it is no wonder if they become snares, toiles, and thorns unto them and that they complain that the streams of their abundance are like the waters of Marah (Ex. 15:23), so bitter that they cannot drink of them, seeing that they want Christ who is the only tree of life to heal them and to change their unpleasing bitterness into a delicious sweetness by the power of His Word.

Providence Does Not Undermine Promises

Secondly, believers are to be cautious that they weaken not the expectation of faith in the performance of any good, which the promise holds forth unto them, by making the providences of

---

2. *ex largitate donantis.*
3. *virtute promiss.*

God that seem to cross the fulfilling of it to be moving arguments to incline them to doubting or diffidence about the truth of it. When Jacob understood that his brother Esau was coming against him with four hundred men (Gen. 32:6), he does not distrust the promise that God had made unto him (Gen. 28:15), but he strongly pleads it as a ground for his deliverance: "Thou saidst, I will surely do thee good, and make thy seed as the sand of the sea, which cannot be numbered for multitude" (Gen. 32:12). When God, by a dream that was doubled on purpose to confirm the certainty of the thing, had revealed unto Joseph the future honor and greatness which he would exalt him unto above his brethren, causing their sheaves to bow to his sheaf, and the sun, moon, and the eleven stars to make obeisance unto him (Gen. 37:7, 9). The means that God uses for the effecting and bringing to pass His decree, not the concurrence of successful and smiling providences, but of such only which to the eye of reason seem rather to destroy the promise than to accomplish it. Who could ever have conceived that the casting of him into a dry pit, the selling of him to the Ishmaelite merchants, the putting of him into prison and fetters by Potiphar as a shameful offender should lead to the advancement of Joseph, and not to his ruin? Can light spring out of darkness, glory out of ignominy, liberty out of thralldom? And yet by such stops as these, God raises up Joseph into the throne of honor. "Until the time that his word came: the word of the LORD tried him," says David (Ps. 105:19).

That is, until the very accomplishment of the promise, he was tried in the expectation of it by many and sore afflictions, in all which he exercised such a measure of faith and patience as not to murmur or repine at the dispensations of God towards him, or faint in his waiting quietly for the fulfilling of the word which the Lord had spoken unto him. "The archers have sorely grieved him, and shot at him, and hated him: But his bow abode in strength, and the arms of his hands were made strong by the hands of the mighty God of Jacob" (Gen. 49:23–24). Therefore, when believers do at any time find the dispensations of God to them in His providences to cross rather than to favor the fulfilling of such promises as He has made to them in His Word, and which they in their prayers do earnestly seek and expect, yet are they not to cast away their confidence, or to take up any such sad conclusions that God has forgotten His promise. [Nor are they to believe] that He bears no respect to them, or their sacrifices, because God does not limit the accomplishment of His promises to the serenity and success of His providences but many times uses such dispensations which seem rather to frustrate and make void His purpose than to establish and effect it. Jonah is set on shore by a whale when the mariners arrive at their port by the ship. The blind man in the gospel, Christ cures by clay and spittle, and not by balsams (John 9:6). And as they that go to sea do not obtain a firm and unmoved state of body by the steadiness of the vessel in a calm but by the accustoming and inuring of themselves to the rollings and tossings of it in several weathers, so neither do believers gain a settled peace of mind by the calm equality of God's providences towards them, but by acquaintance with vicissitudes and adverse revolutions in the midst of which they still find the promise to be as an anchor sure and firm, and, therefore, are not perplexed or amazed at all other changes that befall them.

Take Heed of Curiosity in Selecting Promises

The fourth cautionary direction to believers is to take heed of a sinful and affected curiosity, so as to esteem only those promises most precious which stand in the Scripture like fruit ungathered and untouched by the hand of common Christians, and are like flowers, as they imagine, not at all smelt and blown upon by any but themselves. As there is a vain affectation in some ministers to decline and wave those Scriptures that have in them the greatest pregnancy to confirm their doctrines, and to set their wits on work, and the texts many times upon the rack to force them to speak to their purpose; that so their notions and conceptions may be looked upon by their auditors as neither vulgar nor common. So, there is a lust of fancy in many Christians of pleasing and delighting themselves in the picking and selecting out such promises as have not come under the observation of others, or have been least used by them in the constant daily recourse which they have had unto them. Now, this vanity and curiosity which thus prevails in many Christians does not only spring from pride, which often begets an affectation of singularity, but it arises also from a false conceit and opinion taken up by them that such promises are more sweet when ruminated upon, and more full when sucked on, being like unto breasts that have had little or none of their milk drawn and taken from them.

1. They conceive them to be more sweet and to affect the soul with a greater of delight. But there is a twofold sweetness and delight: the one arises from the goodness of the object, the other from the newness of the object. The newness of the object is that with which fancy is chiefly delighted, and by which it works upon the will to close with it, as a convenient and suitable good. But the understanding propounds the goodness and truth of the object to the will, and thereby draws and wins in to a liking and full embracing of it. Now that which should endear the promise unto believers is not any suggestion from fancy that none but themselves have either observed or used this or that particular promise; and upon that ground to hug it in their bosoms as scholars do those notions and books which none are possessed of but themselves. But the high estimation which they have of them should wholly arise from that transcendent goodness and truth which is in the promises, and makes them deservedly to be of all desired and accepted. Thus Paul commends the gospel, "This is a faithful saying, and worthy of

all acceptation, that Christ Jesus came into the world to save sinners" (1 Tim. 1:15).

2. They conceive, though fondly, them to be more full, as well as more sweet. But this is one of the peculiar excellencies of the promises, that the emanations of comfort which flow from them are not in the least impaired or diminished by the common and daily use of them, no more than light is wasted in the sun by the multitudes of generations that have enjoyed the use and benefit of it. Still, it has as much light in the body of it as it had in its first creation. And so the promises which Abraham, Isaac, and all the faithful descended from them, have successively used and lived upon still retain the same vigor and abound with as great plenty of support and comfort unto present believers as ever they did unto them. As the bee does with an innocent theft, as Parisiensis[4] calls it, sucks honey from the flowers, without the least prejudice to their beautiful colors which delight the eye, or to the fragrant scent which affects the smell of him that gathers them, so believers draw from the promises a grateful satiety both of delight and comfort, without the least diminution of their fullness or sweetness. He that is last in the application of the same promise, may find it as rich in its plenty, as effectual in its vigor, as he that came first unto it. "Wells," says Basil,[5] "are the better and more pure the oftener they be drawn"; and so the promises, which are the wells of salvation, receive an improvement by the frequent and common use of them.

The end of this caution is no way to forbid any Christians valuing or esteem of one particular promise above others, which God, by the powerful workings of His Spirit, has in a special manner made use of for the quieting of their souls in the time of

---

4. John of Paris (ca.1255–1306), Dominican friar, philosopher, and theologian.

5. Basil of Caesarea (329–379), an early Cappadocian church father who fought for the doctrine of the Trinity against the Arians.

their greatest perplexity, and the filling of them with all joy and peace in believing, as if thereby they did derogate ought from the just worth of other promises. For it being God's manner not to seal and manifest His love unto believers by one and the same promise but to make use of this promise to one, and of a differing promise to another, who both lie under the same distress. It is their duty to have in a peculiar remembrance that promise and Scripture above others by which God was pleased first to speak peace to their souls. But the aim of the caution is to keep believers from putting any disrespect upon the precious promises by their esteeming of them to be so much the less worth by how much the more common and ordinary they have been in their use. Did manna nourish the Israelites the less because it was their usual food in the wilderness, or quails the more because they were a new kind of meat? The one indeed pleased their appetite and palate more, but the other supplied their necessities as well. And so the promises which are most obvious and common in their use yield to Christians as much real and solid comfort when rightly applied, though others which they conceive to have been less observed, or by themselves only taken notice of, may more affect and please the curiosity of a lustful fancy.

Take Heed of Carnal Reasonings

The fifth cautionary direction is to take heed of carnal reasonings which are restless in their enmity to all matters that appertain to faith, or at the best full of impotency and unable to yield any assistance to believers in them.

Unwearied Opposition to Faith

First, carnal reason is unwearied in its opposing and contradicting of faith, which of all graces has the most immediate relation unto the promises, and is of greatest use in the application of them. It is an enemy to the first implantation of it, and hinders men from submitting to the righteousness of God, by possessing their minds with unjust prejudices and cavils against His Word. God says that His words do good to them that walk uprightly (Mic. 2:7). But the language of carnal men is: "It is vain to serve God: and what profit is it that we have kept his ordinance…?" (Mal. 3:14). Christ says that His yoke is easy and His burden light (Matt. 11:30). But His carnal disciples cry out, "This is an hard saying; who can hear it?" (John 6:60). God says His waves are just and equal. But the carnal Israelites are not afraid to censure His as crooked and their own as straight (Ezek. 33:17). And, as by the disguises and artifices of carnal reason, men are kept from a happy change of their natural estate by believing; so when faith is wrought, they are by the enmity of the same principle continually disquieted and interrupted in the comfortable enjoyment of those many blessed privileges which they are interested in by faith. Sometimes, it calls into question their title to what they possess and suggests unto them that they are rather presumptuous intruders than just proprietaries, that the evidences upon which they build their hopes are the delusions and self-flatteries of their own hearts and not the unerring testimony of God's Spirit. Sometimes, it raises jealousies concerning the promises themselves, that they are things as easily revoked as they are made, which though they yield present comfort yet do not ascertain any future security, that though God turn not away from them, nor repent Him of His love, yet they may turn from Him and so nullify the promises and the covenant of His mercy unto themselves. It is, therefore, of great concernment unto believers in the making use of the promises to be cautious in admitting the pleas and arguments of carnal reason, which being never so often answered will never be silent. But peremptorily to resolve to believe, notwithstanding all that sense and reason can suggest to the contrary; [that is,] to wink and believe, to shut their eyes against all difficulties. And when they are so great as to pose their reason not to let them to pose their faith. Excellent is that saying of Luther: "In Paradise, Satan first opened our eyes, and now it is our chief labor to shut and fast close them again, that so we may no more be betrayed by them."[6] Sense and reason, being in the things of faith, "a harmful beast,"[7] as he calls it, to overturn and destroy whatever faith uses as a prop to rest itself upon.

Enemy to Faith

Secondly, as carnal reason is an enemy unto faith, so at the best it is full of impotency and unable to give the least assistance to believers in their making use of the promises, or dijudication of spiritual objects, as may appear in three particulars.

1. It is dim-sighted, and wants a perceptive faculty. Busy and curious it is in prying and looking into the mysteries of faith but altogether weak and unskillful in making any true judgment concerning them. Reason is like the crocodile which is reported to be of quick sight on the land but of dull sight on the water. It is sagacious in earthly things but has no insight in spiritual objects. Asaph attempted by the discussions of reason to have found out the ground of God's differing administrations towards His people, and the men of the world, whose bellies were filled with hid treasure, but he was by his own confession soon at a loss: "When I thought to know this, it was too painful for me" (Ps. 73:16).

And when he did go that way to satisfy himself, how opposite is the inference and conclusion to that which he makes upon a second view and looks upon the same things by the light of the lamp of the sanctuary? When he beholds God's dispensations

---

6. *Aperuit nobis in Paradiso oculos Satan, nunc omnis labor in eo nobis est, ut eos iterum claudamus et obturemus.*

7. *noxiabestia.*

with the eye of his reason only, what a wild and erroneous conclusion he takes up: "Verily I have cleansed my heart in vain, and washed my hands in innocency" (v. 13). But when he comes to read them over again by the eye of faith, then he draws a right inference from the premises: "It is good for me to draw near to God" (v. 28).

And as reason is blind in discerning spiritual objects, so is it also unskillful in the use of those means by which faith is enabled to make a full and perfect discovery of them. Reason is like unto a man that takes the wrong end of the perspective glass to see, with which lessens the magnitude of the object, and increases the distance. It looks upon the promises by unapt mediums which do not make a just representation of them, and therefore discerns little or nothing of their reality and existence. But faith that looks at the right end of the glass, which being more full of light multiplies the species and thereby takes away the remoteness of the objects and presents them as close unto the eye. Thus, Abraham saw Christ's day and rejoiced to see it (John 8:56). Great was the space of time between the making of that promise and the fulfilling of it unto Abraham, that in him all the families of the earth should be blessed (Gen. 12:3). But yet his faith, eyeing the power and truth of God that made it, looks upon the long interval of many ages that was between him and his promised seed as upon a very small and inconsiderable distance. Thus, the holy Patriarchs did not only see the promises afar off, but they also saluted and embraced them as near; they were in regard of their own existence afar off, but in regard of their faith, they were hard at hand (Heb. 11:13).

2. Carnal reason, as it is blind, so is it also full of impatience, and, therefore, unmeet to be an assistance unto faith. The apostle tells the believing Hebrews that they have need of patience, that, after they have done the will of God, they might receive the promise (Heb. 10:36). It is so necessary a grace for Christians

that without patience we can scarce be men, much less Christians. The difficulties that believers are to wrestle with are neither few nor small, but sharp, long, and numerous, all which must be endured with patience before they can reap the promise. Though the end be a throne of glory, a crown of life, yet the way is a way of blood; though the reward be sure, yet the waiting for it is long. Now cranial reason is full of impatience; it can neither wait the time nor endure the trials which must be undergone. It likes well of the end but not of the way; it affects the enjoyment of the promise, but it cannot stay the appointed time. Thus, the Israelites gladly embraced the first ridings of their deliverance brought unto them by Moses and Aaron, and with bowed heads worshipped the Lord who had looked upon their afflictions (Ex. 4:31), yet they could not, with patience for a few days, quietly wait [for] the Lord's season. Pharaoh deals more hardly with them than before, and now all their hopes of liberty are at an end; and they complain unto Moses that they were so far from deliverance that he had made them to be abhorred in the eyes of Pharaoh, and in the eyes of his servants, and had put a sword in their hands to slay them (Ex. 5:21). And though Moses was sent to comfort them a second time, and to assure them that the day of their deliverance was at hand, yet for anguish of spirit they hearkened not unto him (Ex. 6:9). Sense and reason do make deaf the ears of believers to whatever God speaks to support them in their trouble, and makes them as unfit to receive any impression from the promise, as water is to take the similitude and character of the seal, which is as soon lost as made. It looks upon a few days as so many years, and a few years as so many ages, and is, therefore, most unmeet to deal in any matters that appertain to faith.

3. Carnal reason is full of groundless fears and jealousies, apt to be discouraged by denials, ready to faint upon the appearance of the least difficulties, and, therefore, unable to contribute any

assistance unto faith, whose peculiar work and art it is to look from and above those impediments which reason stumbles at. Faith is a most venturous grace, which walks upon those deep seas with delight, that the line of reason cannot fathom; when it like unto a young swimmer dares go no further, then it can feel the bottom. Faith gathers resolution from denials and repulses like unto the wheel in the water which being driven from it by the stream returns upon it with the greater violence. When reason sits down disconsolate, and says all pleadings and strivings are in vain. Thus, the woman of Canaan (Matt. 15), from the silence of Christ, from the denials of Christ, from his calling of her dog, finds ground to continue her suit. When He is silent and answers not, then there is hope, because He denies not. When He denies her, then there is more hope, because He speaks, and may quickly be entreated, though at present He deny. When He calls her dog, then her hope arises higher, because though the children only must be full fed, yet surely He will not let the dogs to starve. Faith is a grace which in the greatest exigencies and straits that can befall a believer loses nothing of its courage and magnanimity but cheerfully bears up in the midst of all. When reason is at a loss through the multiplicity of fears, and distractions with which it is filled; the one is like to the timorous passenger in a storm at sea, who makes it his only work to tell the waves, and to shriek at the beating of every billow against the ship; the other is like the industrious pilot who has his hand to the helm, and his eye to heaven,[8] and minds more his duty than his danger. Thus Habakkuk: "Although the fig tree shall not blossom, neither shall fruit be in the vines; the labour of the olive shall fail, and the fields shall yield no meat; the flock shall be cut off from the fold, and there shall be no herd in the stalls: Yet I will rejoice in the LORD, I will joy in the God of my salvation"

---

8. *manum ad clavum, et oculum ad coelum.*

(Hab. 3:17–18). Thus, Job is in the divine record as famous for his confidence, as for his patience, which, in his conflict with God Himself, he will not let go: "Though he slay me, yet will I trust in him" (Job 13:15). Though he breathe out his life, yet shall not his hope expire with it. Oh, therefore, let Christians, when they are to act faith in the promises take heed of the suggestions of carnal reason, and learn to do as they who level at a mark are used to do, who close one eye that they may take aim the better with the other! Shut fast the eye of depraved reason that they may see the more clearly with the eye of faith.

CHAPTER 11

Fanciful Expectations and Settling for Less

Take Heed of Groundless Fancies concerning the Manner of Receiving Comfort

The sixth cautionary direction is to take heed of groundless and wild fancies concerning the manner of receiving comfort, and establishment from the promises so as to expect that the consolations which come from them must be administered rather by the hand of an angel than of a minister, and witnessed by some voice from heaven than by the clear testimony of the Word. And if they come not attended with such pomp and state, then to look upon them as common and ordinary comforts but not as evidences that have a sufficiency of glory and luster to confirm the soul in the love of God. When Naaman the Assyrian came to the prophet Elisha to be cured of his leprosy, he only sent out a messenger unto him who bade him go and wash seven times in Jordan, and flesh should come again unto him, and he should be clean (2 Kings 5:10). But Naaman thought that the prophet would have used more likely means to have wrought the cure, that he himself would have come out unto him that he would strike his hand on the place and call on the name of the Lord his God, and, therefore, departs in anger as scorning the simplicity of the means which was enjoined him. So many Christians, when they lie under deep agonies and perplexities of heart, and are counseled to act faith upon the promises to attend upon the dispensations of the gospel in the Word, to wrestle with God in prayer, they are ready to think that these are salves that may do well for common sores; but their maladies are such that unless Christ touch them with His own hand, the virtue that comes from these things, as from His garments, can never heal them; unless God do from heaven confirm His promises by extraordinary signs and miracles, their breaches and ruptures will never be healed, their comforts and peace will never prevail against their fears and darkness. It is not the prophet's staff laid upon the face of the dead child that will bring life again into it (2 Kings 4:31–34); he must come and stretch himself upon the child ere the flesh of it will wax warm.

This caution is the more necessary to be heeded upon a double ground. First, because of the aptness that is in troubled Christians to affect new means above the right means and to build their confidence upon something that is without the compass of the Word, rather than upon the Word itself. Secondly, in regard of the great danger and deceit that is in those extraordinary ways, by which many pretend to have their comfort and assurance to be confirmed unto them, which in the use of all other means they could never find to be fully and satisfyingly evidenced unto them.

Apt to Try New Ways
First, there is a pronity[1] in Christians especially when exercised with fears and doubts concerning their condition, to grow weary of using such means in which they find not their expectations speedily answered, and through an over-hasty desire of comfort to try the gaining of it in a new way, rather than to persevere in the old, being in this not much unlike to many weak and crazy patients that are more ready to fancy every new medicine they

---

1. *pronity*: inclination.

hear of, and to tamper with it, than to expect a recovery by going through a course of physic prescribed by the physician. Gregory[2] tells of a religious lady of the empress's bedchamber, whose name was Gregoria, that being much troubled about her salvation did write unto him that she would never cease importuning him till he had sent her word that he had received a revelation from heaven that she was saved. To whom he returned this answer: that it was a hard and altogether useless matter which she required of him.[3] It was difficult for him to obtain, being unworthy to have the secret counsels of God to be imparted unto him; and it was unprofitable for her to know not only for the reason which he assigns, that such a revelation might make her too secure, but also because it was impossible for him to demonstrate and make known unto her, or any other, the truth and infallibility of the revelation which he had received to be from God; so that had she afterwards called into question the truth of it, as well she might, her troubles and doubts concerning her salvation would have been as great as they were before. O, therefore, let believers that would be confirmed in the peace and love of God take heed of relinquishing that more sure word of prophecy which shines as a light in a dark place (2 Peter 1:19), and of flying unto visions, revelations, voices from heaven, to assure and evidence unto them their salvation, and to be the seals of the truth of those comforts and joys which they are filled with. These are ways that have more external glory and pomp in them, but the acting of faith on the promises, and the adhering of the soul unto those truths declared in them, is the unquestionable way of obtaining a full establishment of heart in all sound joy and peace; and, therefore, Luther, though, as he confesses, he was often tempted

---

2. Gregory the Great (ca. 540–604), Pope, founder of the medieval papacy, and architect of the Gregorian Mission to convert Anglo-Saxons to Christianity.

3. *Rem difficilem postulas, et inutilem.*

to ask for signs, apparitions, revelations from heaven, to confirm him in his way, yet tells how strongly he did withstand them: "I have," says he, "indented[4] with the Lord my God that he would never send me dreams, visions, [or] angels; for I am well-content with this gift, that I have the Holy Scripture, which abundantly teaches and supplies all necessaries for this life, and that also which is to come."[5]

Danger and Deceit of New Ways
Secondly, as there is an aptness in Christians to affect such extraordinary ways and means of comfort, so is there also no little danger and deceit in the ways themselves.

1. They are dangerous in regard that they make the Word and promises to be as things of little value and esteem, which should be as the only sacred Oracles of truth for believers to have their recourse unto. Such who cry up revelations make it their practice to cry down the Word, and look upon those that adhere to the Scriptures, and make them the touchstone to try every spirit by, as having little or no acquaintance with the deep things of God.[6] Such who affirm assurance to be the immediate voice of the Spirit speaking in them, and saying unto them that their sins are forgiven them, how disdainfully do they speak of the certainty and persuasion which believers have from the gracious operations of the Spirit, and the blessed fruits of holiness wrought by Him in their souls, which by His enlightening they are enabled to discern and thereby to be confidently persuaded of God's love unto them, and of their interest in all the promises? This they

---

4. *indent*: to covenant.

5. *Pactum feci cum Domino Deo meo, ne mihi mittat vel visiones, vel somnia, veleliam Angelos. Contentus enim sum hoc dono, quod habeo Scripturam sanctam, quae abunde docet ac suppeditat omnia, quae necessaria sunt, tum ad hanc vitam, tum ad futuram.*

6. *vocalistas, et literatistas*, vowalists and letterists.

dignify with no better or higher title than a humane faith, than a conjectural knowledge, though the testimony be truly supernatural both in regard of the efficient cause and also of the means whereby they come to be thus persuaded. Yea, though it be the only safe way which the Scripture holds out for believers to try their estates by, to look unto the effects and fruits of the Spirit of God in them, and not to any immediate voices or revelations from heaven, as the testimony of God's love unto them; yet do such vilify this kind of evidence as low and carnal, and altogether unmeet for evangelical Christians to make use of. What should they need to have a rushlight to see by when they may enjoy the sun which is the light of lights?

2. As they are dangerous, so are they full of deceit and illusion. Young Samuel, not acquainted with any extraordinary manifestations of the presence and power of God, took the voice of God from heaven to be the voice of old Eli (1 Sam. 3:5). And so do many take the irregular motions of their own hearts to be the divine breathings, and the powerful impulses of the Spirit of God, whereby they are stirred up to the undertaking of sundry actions which the Word in the least measure countenances not. How frequently in these times do fanatic persons baptize the violent workings of their own distempered fancies with the name of the visions of God and of the raptures of the Spirit? How often does Satan by transforming himself into an angel of light endeavor the seducement and ruin of many Christians, against whom as an angel of darkness he could not prevail, being in everything God's ape to imitate those extraordinary ways by which God has sometimes made known Himself unto His people? Gerson[7] in his book *De probation spirituum* [1415], of

---

7. John Gerson (1363–1429), Chancellor of the University of Paris, and a well-known medieval theologian. He was one of the first theologians to develop a theory of natural rights, and wrote numerous theological tracts.

the trial of spirits, tells a remarkable story of Satan's appearing to a holy man in a most glorious and beautiful manner, professing himself to be Christ, and because he for his exemplary holiness was worthy to be honored above others, therefore, he appeared unto him; but the old man readily answered him that he desired not to see his Savior in this wilderness; it should suffice him to see Him hereafter in heaven, and withal added this pithy prayer, "O, let thy sight be my reward, Lord, in another life, and not in this life."[8]

This direction, therefore, is of no little importance unto believers that would not lose and wilder themselves in uncertainties both in regard of duty and comfort to take heed how they leave the precept of the Word, and betake themselves unto revelations for the guidance of their ways, or how they neglect the application of the promises by faith for the establishing of their hearts in the peace and love of God, and expect their assurance to flow from an immediate voice or dictate of the Spirit, as if the Word and promises had no activity and light in them to evidence and declare the certainty and truth of these things unto their souls. Such ways, though the novelty of them may render them pleasing to many, yet it cannot, as we see, make them safe to any that tread or walk in them. And, therefore, let that of Augustine be every Christian's practice and prayer: "Lord, let thy Holy Scriptures be my pure delights, in which I can neither deceive or ever be deceived."[9]

Let Not Your Heart Out on Earthly Objects

The seventh and last cautionary direction is to take heed of having the heart let out to earthly objects, either in earnest desires after them, or in long and frequent musings of the mind upon

---

8. *Sit in alio seculo, non in hoc, visio tua merces mea.*

9. *Sint sacrae Scripturae tue deliciae meae, in quibus nec possim fallere nec falli.*

them. The application of the promises is then most powerful and operative when they lie nearest and closest unto the soul; and the comforts that distill from them are then most sweet when they are received into the most inward parts of the hidden man. The softest garments men usually wear next [to] their skin, and the best jewels they lay up in the most inward cells of their cabinets. And of such a nature are the promises and invitations of mercy in the gospel; they are things of the greatest delicacy, and, therefore, should be applied next unto the heart, which is of all parts the most tender. They are of the highest worth and value, and therefore should highest be lodged in the most retired and inward receptacles of the mind as their most due and proper seat. All interposition of earthly things does not only hinder the conveyance both of grace, and comfort from the promises, but also according to the measure and predominancy of it makes the heart as an unmeet vessel to receive such heavenly treasure in divers respects.

They Fill the Heart

First, earthly things fill the heart, and thereby put it into an incapacity of receiving either divine counsel or comfort from the Word or promises. They fill the heart with crowds of businesses so that Christ and His Word find no more place in it than He and His mother did room in the inn where the manger was fain to be His cradle (Luke 2:7). They fill the heart with diversity of cares and solicitudes so that it cannot have any freedom to attend heavenly duties. Martha, who was troubled about many things, did not with Mary, her sister, sit at Christ's feet to hear the Word, her cumber[10] about much serving made her to neglect the one thing that was needful (Luke 10:38–42). They many times fill the heart with pride and scorn, so as that the choicest

---

10. *cumber*: to be overwhelmed.

things of the gospel are no better than foolishness. The Pharisees heard Christ preach against earthly affections, but they derided him (Luke 16:14). The full soul loathes the honeycomb (Prov. 27:7), and so an earthly mind rejects the Word, which is more sweet than the dropping honey.

They Defile the Heart

Secondly, earthly things defile the heart with many vile and corrupt affections, which unqualify it for the reception of holy and precious promises. They stain the heart with an adulterous and impure love, which is enmity unto God (James 4:4), and make it apt to prefer carnal satisfactions before communion with Christ. They defile the heart with a false and unsound confidence, turning it from God who is the sole object of trust, unto the mutable and unstable creature; and, therefore, Paul enjoins Timothy to charge them that are rich in this world that they trust not in uncertain riches but in the living God (1 Tim. 6:17). They pollute the heart with sensual joys, [and] with unhallowed pleasures and delights, so that the joy of the corn, wine, and oil increasing extinguishes that complacency and tranquility of mind that flows from the presence and fruition of spiritual objects, as in luxurious persons strange love eats out and obliterates that which is conjugal. How then can any man expect that the Holy Spirit of promise should be both a Counselor and Comforter unto such a one, whose love, confidence, joys, are adulterate and sinful? Surely, He who has the purity of a dove will never take up the lodging of a crow; He who dwells in the soul when it is a temple of holiness will never afford His presence when it is turned into a cage of unclean birds.

They Divide the Heart

Thirdly, earthly objects divide the heart (Hos. 2:10), and make it uncertain in its motions towards God. As the balance has no steadfastness in itself, but does by every breath and touch fluctuate, sometimes to the one hand, sometimes to the other, so the earthly mind is various and inconstant in its desires to heavenly things, sometimes for a short and sudden fit it seems to affect them, and by and by grows cold and heartless again. Like to the grasshoppers, which, as Gregory observes, give a flirt up, and make a faint essay of flying towards heaven, and then presently falls on the earth again. Thus the young man (Mark 10:17) comes running to Christ to show his fervor and zeal, kneels to Him to testify his observance, prays to Him to direct him in the way to eternal life to evidence his care and solicitude about it; but when Christ bids him to sell whatsoever he had and give to the poor that so he might have treasure in heaven, how soon does he who ran and kneeled and prayed to Christ turn his back upon Him and go from Him? How quickly are his desires turned into sorrow, and his prayer into a fearful apostasy? Now then, if earthly things do make the heart thus unsteadfast and unfaithful to God, how exceedingly must they needs indispose it for the reception of grace and comfort from God in all His promises, to the obtaining of which nothing is more requisite than an evenness and constancy of the desires in seeking after them, and an entireness and oneness of heart in laying hold on them? For as all the promises are one in Christ, and cannot be severed or parted, no more than lines in their common center, so neither must the heart by which they are embraced be divided. Whole Christ and all His promises are given to every believer, and are no otherwise diversified than according to the exigence of men's present conditions, which sometimes requires the application of one promise, and sometimes of another; and, therefore, must the whole heart be given unto Him again, or else we cannot ever expect to have any interest in Him or His blessed promises. True it is that in the best of Christians, there is found an unsteadfastness of heart and affections, but it is not an unsteadfastness in respect of the object but only in degrees. It is not such as distracts the heart and makes it to float between two different objects but only makes it unequal in its motions towards one and the same thing. As the bowl when it is first thrown out of the hand runs more swiftly towards the mark than it does afterwards, but yet the tendency of the motion is the same, though the vigor and strength of it be not alike. So believers, when partakers of some fresh gales of the Spirit, do then move towards Christ with more quick and lively affections than at other times, but yet by that inward principle of holiness that is within them, they are always carried towards Him in their desires, though not after one equal and uniform manner.

This caution, therefore, though it be the last, yet is it not the least, which believers are with much diligence and circumspection to observe that would gladly be partakers of the spiritual riches and treasures which are in the promises. But the end of it is not that we should abandon all care and industry in our callings, or that we should affect a voluntary and monkish poverty, as if there were an absolute inconsistency between having the blessings of this life and the enjoyments of the other life. We may possess earthly comforts, but we must not be possessed by them. We may use them as flowers to smell on, but not as garlands to crown ourselves with them. We may in our pilgrimage walk with them as staves in our hands, seeking a country which is above, but we may not load ourselves with them, and bear them as burdens upon our backs. We may make them our encouragements, but not our confidence. We may mind them as our accessories, but we may not love them as our principal happiness. As bees, though they live in the midst of their cells of honey and wax, yet have not their wings touched with any viscous matter that may hinder their delightful flight abroad and their nimble passing from one flower to another. So should Christians that live in the abundance of earthly comforts, as in an hive of sweetness, be exceeding careful that nothing of the world cleaves to their affections, which are the wings of the soul, that may hinder the lifting and raising up of their hearts towards heavenly objects or abate the activity of their thoughts in their frequent musings on the promises and other mysteries of the gospel on which the mind above all other things ought to be most exercised and delighted.

I have now done with the third particular that in the entrance of this task was propounded to be handled, and have insisted longer upon every direction both positive and cautionary than I first intended, but my end was not to offend any by prolixity but to render them more useful and necessary unto all than otherwise they might have been if contracted into a less and narrower compass and made like unto the description of a pitched field or battle wherein there are many heads and spears painted but few or no complete and entire bodies.

CHAPTER 12

Faith Is Not Full Assurance

I come now to the fourth particular which consists of divers queries together with their resolutions, the clear answering of which will much facilitate the use and application of the promises. And the first query is whether the essence of saving and justifying faith lies in a prevailing assurance so as that he who truly believes does certainly know himself to have faith and to believe on Christ.

This question I do the rather choose to speak somewhat unto in regard that many of our divines have in their writings not distinguished between faith, affiance,[1] and assurance,[2] but have promiscuously treated of them as if they were one and the same thing. Yea, sundry pious and learned men have defined faith to be a full persuasion of the heart grounded on the promises of God. Now that which chiefly led them to give this definition of faith was their zeal to maintain the certainty and evidence of faith against popish doubts. But a good intention will no more make a truth than a fair mark will make a good shoot, for while on the one hand they have endeavored to vindicate faith from that languor and uncertainty unto which the papists have subjected it,

---

1. *affiance*: trust
2. *fides, fiducia,* and *certituda.*

they have on the other hand occasioned great fears and perplexities to arise in the hearts of many tender and weak Christians who are apt to use this as an argument against themselves, that they have no faith at all because they have no assurance at all. To keep, therefore, such bruised reeds from being broken, and the smoking flax from being quenched under the sense of their want of assurance, I shall by sundry demonstrations clearly show that the essence of saving faith does not stand in a prevailing assurance, that a believer may have the one and yet want the other.

The Poor Estate of the Blessed

The first shall be taken from that estate and condition of men whom Christ the great Judge of all the world pronounces and declares to be blessed; and they are such as are believers, because all blessedness under the gospel comes only by faith; and this blessedness stands in the forgiveness of sins (Rom. 4:6–7). Yet, their present condition speaks nothing less than assurance: "Blessed are the poor in spirit," says our Savior (Matt. 5:3). So again, "Blessed are they that mourn" (v. 4). And again, "Blessed are they which do hunger and thirst after righteousness" (v. 6). But spiritual poverty, mourning, hunger, though they be gospel-graces which arise from faith are all together distinct from assurance, as may appear in their different effects. Assurance is riches and not poverty (Col. 2:2), joy and not mourning (1 John 1:4), satisfaction and not hunger of want and emptiness (Ps. 90:14). So in that parable of the Pharisee and the publican going up into the temple to pray (Luke 18:10–11), our Savior tells us that the Pharisee was full of presumption and false confidence; but the publican, through a sense of his unworthiness, was almost overwhelmed with fears and misgivings of heart; he stands afar off, and dares not draw near; he is so full of shame as that he would not so much as lift up his eyes to heaven. He smites his breast, as pointing out the fountain from whence all his misery and sin did flow. He accuses himself in his prayer as a great sinner. In all his actions, gestures, words there is no expression of his assurance of pardon; and yet he went away justified, and not the other, which without faith he could not have been.

The State of Desertion

A second demonstration is from the state of desertion into which a believer may fall. A child of light may walk in darkness (Isa. 50:10), and neither behold the sunlight of God's countenance, nor the starlight of his own graces for many days. He may be as a tree in winter whose sap is wholly retired to the root, and has neither fruit nor leaves hanging on it to evidence that it is not dead. As in the sufferings of Christ upon the cross, there was for a time a withdrawing of the light of God's countenance,[3] but not any breaking or dissolution of the union.[4] So in the derelictions that a believer is subject unto, there may be a separation in regard of the comfortable manifestation and shining forth of the beams of God's love, but no interruption in regard of his union with Christ. Thus it was with David (Ps. 51:12), who begs the restoration of the joy of God's salvation, and the establishment of His free Spirit. And thus it was with Heman (Ps. 88), who, in his own apprehension, was as one free among the dead (v. 5). Thus it was with Jonah, when lying in the belly of the whale, as in a grave, he said, "I am cast out of thy sight" (Jonah 2:4). But yet still they were believers, and their faith was alive at the root, neither was there any intercision of their fellowship with Christ. Now if faith, when assurance is lost, continues as [a] believer's union with Christ, it will also begin his union with Christ, though it be not accompanied with assurance. Or, if a

---

3. *subtractio visionis.*
4. *dissolutio unionis.*

believer may lose his assurance, and yet not wholly lose his faith, then may he also have faith before it grows up into assurance.

Differing Conditions of Believers

A third demonstration is taken from the differing stature and condition of believers. As in the world, there are not only aged men whose multitude of years do teach wisdom, and young men whose bones being moistened with marrow are full of strength, but there are also infants which hang upon the breast of their mother, who, though they enjoy life, yet do not know that they have life, or are able to reflect upon any action which they do. So, in the church, there are not only Mnasons that are old disciples [Acts 21:16], experienced in the mysteries of the gospel, and young Timothys that are trained up in the knowledge of the Scriptures, but there are also newborn babes (1 Peter 2:2) who are partakers of a spiritual life, and yet are not able to apprehend that they have eternal life given unto them. There are in the fold of Christ not only sheep which He leads forth into green pastures, but there are also lambs which He gathers with His arm and carries in His bosom, a place both of safety, and of warmth (Isa. 40:11). Now, if the essence of faith did lie in assurance, and that none did believe but they that did know they do believe, this distinction and difference between Christians would be of little or no use. If all that are believers exercise the reflex acts of faith, as well as the direct, in what should the babe in Christ differ from the grown man? Wherein should the bruised reed be distinguished from the established cedar? How should the thirsty and wearied soul that dares not deny Christ to be his, and yet cannot say that certainly He is his, be comforted? How should the sinking and well-nigh despairing Christian that cries out [that] he has no saving faith, because [he has] no assurance, have doubts and objections comfortably answered? What use would there be of signs and marks which the Scripture gives as a staff into the hands of weak ones to support and stay them up if faith stands in a full persuasion of God's love to a man's self in particular? St. John's whole epistle, which was written for this end, that believers might know that they had eternal life (1 John 5:13), would be to no purpose if faith itself did consist in the knowledge of their having it.

The Object of Saving Faith

A fourth demonstration is taken from the object of saving and justifying faith, which is the person of Christ, and not any maxim or proposition which is the object of assurance. That on which the chief act of justifying faith is exercised that is the primary object of faith. But the main act of faith is to unite Christ and a believer together, for by being one with Him we come to be justified by Him and not otherwise. Now, that which makes this union on the believer's part is the adherence and cleaving of the soul unto Christ as the greatest and chiefest good. As the lustful and evil eye by looking upon a woman makes such a union with her in his heart and affections as that thereby he is judged by our Savior to be guilty of adultery (Matt. 5:28), so the seeing of the fullness of Christ, and the true desire of enjoying Him, is such a marriage-glance as makes a tie and union between Christ and the soul that thus looks towards Him for life and salvation.

Answering Objections

But it may be objected, if faith be not assurance, and a persuasion in particular that Christ is mine, wherein lies the application of faith which divines do so much urge and contend for against the papists? To answer this objection, it is granted that the popish faith which stands in a bare general assent unto the promises and the truths which are revealed in the gospel is wholly insufficient to salvation and that there is necessarily required to an effectual and saving faith a special and particular application as has been formerly showed. But there is a twofold application: the one is axiomatical, and the other is real. The axiomatical application is that which assurance makes, whereby a believer is enabled to say, "Christ is mine." The real application [that] faith makes in which, though a believer cannot say that Christ is his, yet he does by an act of recumbency cast himself upon Christ for salvation, and resolves neither to seek it nor expect it any other way. Thus, the prodigal (Luke 15:18), did cast himself upon his father when he could not tell whether he would own him as his son, or make him so much as a hired servant.

But secondly, it may be objected, if faith be not assurance, wherein lies the certainty of faith? To this I answer that there is a double certainty: the one is a certainty of sense, such as Thomas had, who seeing believed (John 20:29). And such a certainty assurance has which is rather a kind of sense than faith. The other is a certainty of event, and this faith has, though it want the former. He that believes shall as certainly not perish as he who is assured, though he does not know it after that manner as the other does. Christ has promised that he who comes to Him, He will in no wise cast out (John 6:37). The words include more than they express. He will be so far from casting out any that come to Him that He will embrace them in the arms of His dearest love and manifest the most tender compassions of His heart towards them.

But the end of all that has been spoken in answer to this query is not that any should rest in their having of faith without assurance, or lessen their giving of all diligence to make their calling and election sure. Though a malefactor may be pardoned and he not know of it, yet he cannot be so comfortable as he that carries his pardon sealed in his bosom. He whom God loves, though he know it not, is happy; but he that knows it knows himself to be happy.

And, therefore, believers, though they are not to faint under the want of assurance, or to conclude against themselves that they have no faith because they have no assurance, yet they ought in prayer and all other ordinances to seek not only the having of eternal life but the knowledge of their having it in Christ.

CHAPTER 13

Promises of Mercy and Pardon

The second query is what use a believer may make of the promises of mercy and pardon after relapses and falling into gross sins which waste the conscience; and whether he may lay an immediate claim unto his right and interest in them without his being first humbled and afflicted for his sins.

To this I answer that though it be not with a believer under the gospel as it was with the Nazarite under the law, who, if he were defiled in the time of his consecration, lost all the former days of his separation and was to begin it wholly anew (Num. 6:12), though he do not by his present defilement lose the virtue of his former cleansing and purifying of himself so as to extinguish his interest in the promises. Yet his right may justly be suspended so that he cannot actually enjoy the benefit and privilege of them until he first humble himself and lay to heart the greatness of his defection and apostasy from God. But that I may give more distinct and clear satisfaction to this question, I shall speak to these two heads. First, I shall show how far a believer may and ought to charge the guilt of atrocious sins that he falls into upon himself. Secondly, I shall show how far he may not go, or conclude any sentence against himself, there being errors oftentimes committed in the excess, as well as in the defect.

How Far a Believer Ought to Censure Himself after Atrocious Sins

First, how far a believer may and ought to judge and sentence himself for sins that are not of daily incursion,[1] and incident to human frailty but are sins that more immediately hazard and endanger salvation[2] itself as springing from more mature deliberation and a more full consent of will; and take it in these particulars.

Acknowledge Just Desert

First, a believer ought to acknowledge that such sins which have in them a notoriety of fact,[3] do deserve a notoriety and exemplariness in their punishment;[4] and he is to be affected as one who has justly merited death, though it be not inflicted, because the desert of sin is still the same, though the sentence be revoked by a pardon. The mercy of a prince is richly manifested in giving unto a traitor his life, but yet that does not disoblige him to confess that his offense deserved death but lays rather a greater tie upon him to do it, that so he may magnify the clemency of his sovereign. So, though God keeps a believer from coming into the condemnation of sinners by giving unto him a royal and full pardon for whatever he has done against Him, yet this ought to be so far from withholding him to acknowledge what the just wages of his rebellions are, as that it ought the more to provoke Him thereunto, that so he may give God the glory of His free pardoning grace. Thus, Peter bewailed the foulness of his sin in denying his Lord and Master (Mark 14:72). We translate it, "He

---

1. *quotidianae incursionis.*
2. *devoratria salutis.*
3. *notorietatem facti.*
4. *notorietatem poenae.*

thought thereon and wept."[5] But Theophylact,[6] and others with him, interpret it, "he covered his head and wept,"[7] alluding to the general custom in the Eastern countries where the condemned malefactors had their faces covered. And by this ceremony Peter judged his sin to have deserved no less than death, and as a son of death he wailed himself: he "wept bitterly" (Luke 22:62).

Acknowledge Unworthiness

Secondly, a believer may so far charge the guilt of gross sins and defections upon himself as to acknowledge his utter unworthiness to stand in any relation of love unto God, and that He might be so far from owning him as a son that He might deny to look upon him in the number of His servants. Thus, the prodigal (whom divines not improbably conceive to be the emblem of a regenerate man falling into scandalous sins), in his return to his father (Luke 15:19), acknowledges himself to be unworthy to be called his son. Though he does not deny the relation of a son, yet he judges himself most unworthy of the title of a son, and thinks it a happiness if he may but be in his house as a hireling. And surely every child of God, who has through loose and riotous living wasted both his grace and his comforts, and brought sad extremities upon himself by straying from his Father's house, ought in those resolutions and purposes of heart, which he has of returning unto God again, to be deeply apprehensive [of] how unworthy he is of any favorable reception from him. [He ought to think of] how undeserving he is to lodge in His house as a servant, much more to lie in His bosom as a son, that thereby he may the better prize the mercy of restored love; and for the future may the more dread the sad effects of a voluntary

---

5. ἐπιβαλὼν ἔκλαιε.

6. Theophylact of Ohrid (1055–1107), Byzantine archbishop and commentator on the Bible.

7. *obvelavit se.*

departure from God and be more watchful in preserving his communion with Him.

Repent and Be Ashamed

Thirdly, a believer falling into scandalous and vile pollutions ought so far to judge himself and to charge the guilt of them upon his soul as not to lay hold immediately upon the promises of forgiveness until he first renew his repentance and be throughly ashamed of the evil of his doings. When Moses interceded for Miriam, whom God had smitten with leprosy, if her father (says the Lord) had but spit in her face, should she not have been ashamed seven days (Num. 12:14)? That is, if her earthly father provoked to anger had expressed his displeasure by spitting upon her, should she not for a season have been sorrowful and pensive? How much more then, when her heavenly Father is displeased by her sin, should she, for a time, be ashamed and shut out from the privileges and society of the congregation? To be guilty of great sins and at the same time without remorse and grief of heart to lay hold on the promises of mercy is not the acting of faith but of presumption, because faith always proceeds according to God's method in the obtaining of peace and comfort. Now, the way by which God speaks peace and makes good the promises of forgiveness is by repentance. And, therefore, till that be renewed, the comfort of pardon is suspended. First, God heard Ephraim bemoaning himself (Jer. 31:18). And then he remembered him; then he manifests the bowels of a tender Father, and says, "I will surely have mercy upon him" (v. 20).

Acknowledge Temporal Affliction as Just

Fourthly, a believer falling into gross and peace-destroying sins is so far to charge the guilt of them upon his soul as to acknowledge that all those temporal afflictions and chastisements, which God as a Father provoked to anger lays upon him, are by his sins justly deserved, and by God righteously inflicted. That God makes His own children to feel the smart of His displeasure in heavy and sore afflictions, occasioned by their iniquities, is a truth which the Scripture holds forth with so much evidence, that he that runs may read it. They rebelled and vexed His Holy Spirit; therefore, He was turned to be their enemy and He fought against them, Isaiah 63:10. So again, "For the iniquity of his covetousness was I wroth, and smote him: I hid me, and was wroth" (Isa. 57:17). What pregnant instances also were old Eli, upon whose person and posterity God brings a most severe and dreadful judgment (1 Sam. 2:31–33)? David, who complains that his sins are a burden too heavy for him (Ps. 38:4), that his wounds stink and are corrupted because of his foolishness (v. 5), that he is feeble and sore broke (v. 8). Jonah, who cries out of the belly of the whale, as out of the belly of hell, that he is forsaken and cast out of God's sight (Jonah 2:2–3). How easy were it by an addition of examples in this kind to make the number to swell into a catalogue? But a taste is enough. Now, what their carriage and behavior towards God is in this condition see it in their expressions: old Eli, when he heard of the judgment of God denounced against him, says, "It is the LORD: let him do what seemeth him good" (1 Sam. 3:18); David under all his pressures acknowledges that in faithfulness He had afflicted him (Ps. 119:75); so Jonah, who had fled from the presence of God, in the prayer that he pours out before Him in his extremity, confesses the sin and vanity of all other dependencies save on God alone: "They that observe lying vanities forsake their own mercies" (Jonah 2:8).

But it may be objected: how can it stand with the justice of God to punish sin in His children with any such kind of affliction [with] Christ having made an absolute and plenary satisfaction for them? To this the answer is easy: these temporal punishments, though they have displeasure mixed with them, yet they do not flow from the vindictive justice of God as an unreconciled enemy but are the corrections of a provoked Father, and wholly differ in the end from the vindictive which are not medicinal but destructive. The judge who sentences the hand of a malefactor to be cut off has not the same end with the physician that cuts off a hand when it is incurably festered: the one commands it as a satisfaction due to justice, the other enjoins it as a means to preserve the safety of the other parts. So, when God afflicts the wicked and believers with the same temporal evils, though the smart and pain may be in both alike, yet He does it not with the same mind, nor to the same end; the one He punishes in order to the satisfaction of His justice, the other, as a Father, He corrects in order to their amendment; to the one, therefore, it is properly a punishment, and to the other truly a medicine.

How Far a Believer Ought Not to Charge Himself with Atrocious Sins

The second head that I am to speak unto is to show how far believers are not to charge the guilt of their great and most heinous sins upon themselves: And this also take in the four following particulars.

Do Not Conclude Loss of Salvation

First, believers are not to charge the guilt of such sins upon themselves, as from thence to conclude that there is an absolute fall from the state of justification and the grace of adoption so as that now they are no longer sons nor have any right to the heavenly inheritance. The love of God in Christ is an endless and unchangeable love (John 13:1), and has its perpetuity founded not upon any thing in us but upon the firm rock of His will and counsel. His covenant is everlasting, ordered in all things and sure, although we be not so with God (2 Sam. 23:5). True it is that the fall and lapses of a justified person do so far make a breach upon his state of justification and adoption that the comforts and privileges of it are thereby withheld and suspended, but his right thereunto is not made null or extinguished. He is under the power of an interdiction but not under the power of an ejection. He may not, like Absalom, see the king's face (2 Sam. 14:24), but he is not an exile. And in this condition, he abides until he renew his repentance and thereby recover a fitness and aptitude to enjoy what before he had a right unto, being like a cleansed leper who has the liberty of returning unto his house from which his defilement had separated him and shut him out. Now, if any think the effects and consequences of this spiritual sequestration imports little, and that they are not antidotes strong enough to check the presumption of the flesh which is in believers, and to keep them from playing the wantons with the grace of God, to such all that I shall say is that to me they seem to be as blind men that understand little or nothing the wide difference between the light of the sun and the darkness of the night; and to have little experience in themselves how sad the condition of that soul is from whom God hides His face or turns his smiles into frowns; and how happy he is in the overflowings of all joy, peace, and comfort, who has the shine of God's face to be the health of his countenance (Ps. 42:11).

Do Not Conclude Former Sins Unforgiven

Secondly, believers are not to charge the guilt of criminal sins into which they fall upon themselves, so as thereby to apprehend or conclude that the pardon of former sins is made void and of none effect. The forgiveness of sins past may aggravate and accent the iniquities that are afterwards committed, being done against the riches of mercy received, but the commission of new sins does not revoke the pardon that was before given, or make the guilt of such sins to return again in their full strength and power. No more than subsequent debts make bonds formerly cancelled and vacated to stand in force. For God, when He pardons, does not insert any conditional clauses that carry a respect to our future conversation, and make the efficacy of His pardon to depend upon our well or ill doing. His gifts and graces are the fruits of His immutable counsel and will, and, therefore, without all repentance it may not be denied, but this truth has divers adversaries: the Lutherans are vehement in their opposition of it, as also the papists and the Arminians. And yet I say they who have skill and leisure to consult the schoolmen who much agitate this question [of] whether sins pardoned ever return and live again[8] in their guilt so as to accuse and to condemn? [You] will find there are more who are for the negative than for the affirmative. But it is not my purpose to enter into the lists and to take up the wasters in this controversy. It is enough that the Scripture expressions concerning God's pardoning of sin clearly hold forth His forgiving of them to be full and absolute: "I have blotted out, as a thick cloud, thy transgressions, and, as a cloud, thy sins" (Isa. 44:22). The cloud that is scattered or dissolved by the sun, though others may succeed it, never returns to make a second appearance, but is wholly extinguished, and, therefore, man's going down into the grave, who never returns unto the land of the living again, is compared unto it (Job 7:9). So Jeremiah 50:20, "the sins of Judah, and they shall not be found: for I will pardon them whom I reserve." So again, Micah 7:19, "Thou wilt cast all their sins into the depths of the sea." Things that are cast into the bottom of the sea never come to sight again but are more surely buried than things that are hid in the grave, and in the bowels of the earth, which may possibly be dug again. What more significant words can be used to declare the absoluteness of God's pardoning sin than these of the prophets?

---

8. *peccata redeant.*

Do Not Conclude Loss of All Grace

Thirdly, believers falling into gross and conscience wasting sins are not to charge the guilt of them upon themselves so as to conclude thereby that they have utterly lost all sanctifying and inherent grace. Such sins may make a believer to be as a man in a swoon who is without all motion, but not as a carcass which is without all life. They may be in his heart as spiders in an hive, which spoil the honey but do not kill the bees; they blast and wither the precious fruits of grace and profession, but they do not wholly destroy the root and principle from whence they flow. Still, the seed of God abides in him (1 John 3:9). The apostasy of Peter in denying our Savior was great. It was a complicated denial; there was in it a denial of so much as knowing Him,[9] and a denial of all communion and converse with Him.[10] And yet in this reiterated defection, the faith of Peter did not expire and give up the ghost. For Christ prayed that his faith might not fail (Luke 22:32). Now, the ground of this indeficiency[11] in grace is not from its own strength, as it is a quality in us, but from the covenant and promise of God, who has said that He will put his fear into our hearts that we shall not depart from Him (Jer. 32:40). He that keeps us by faith, keeps faith itself in us.[12]

This particular is very necessary for such Christians to think upon, who, after a falling into some foul sin, do not only mourn over their folly, as they justly ought, but are apt also to complain that heretofore indeed they had some good in them; a little faith they could by some effects discern in themselves, a spark of love to God was once kindled in their breasts. But now, alas, all is utterly extinct and lost! Now they are in no better condition than in the gall of bitterness, and the bonds of iniquity, a rude

---

9. *negatio notitiae.*
10. *negatio consortii.*
11. *indeficiency*: unfailing.
12. *Qui custodit nos per fidem, costodit in nobis ipsam fidem.*

and deformed chaos of sin and folly, without any principle of grace or appearance of beauty. And in thus doing, they do not only heighten their present darkness and trouble but also are injurious unto the promise and faithfulness of God, who has fixed grace in the heart of a believer more firmly than the soul is seated in the body, which is subject to death and dissolution.

Do Not Conclude Loss of All Comfort

Fourthly, believers are not so to charge the guilt of their great sins upon themselves as from thence to infer any such sad conclusions as these: that they never shall enjoy any day or hour of comfort again but walk in continual darkness, or that they shall never be used any more as instruments of service, or be a vessel unto honor meet for the Master's use, but be as the broken shards that are not fit to take fire from the hearth, or to take water out of the pit (Isa. 30:14). That they who defile themselves with voluntary and gross sins, if we look unto the just merit of them, deserve to be so dealt with it cannot be denied. But that God retaliates the sins of His children with such dealings though they be deeply humbled for their apostasy, and with strong cries beg both pardon and acceptance from Himself is contrary not only to the promises of mercy, which He has made to penitent sinners (Jer. 3:12), but also to many pregnant instances of such whom He has both comforted with His love and highly honored with His service. With what expressions and demonstrations of affection is the dejected prodigal received by his father who "gives to his straying son kisses and not blows,"[13] says Chrysologus?[14] No food is too good to satisfy his hunger, no raiment too costly to clothe him with, no ornament too precious to adorn him. The

---

13. *peccanti filio dat oscula, non flagella.*

14. Peter Chrysologus (406–450), Bishop of Ravenna, known as the "Doctor of Homilies" for his powerful preaching and deep reflections on the biblical text.

fatted calf, the best robe, the ring of gold are the sure pledges of his father's love (Luke 15). What a choice vessel of honor and service was Peter after his fall, who was honored with the dispensation of the gospel and had his labors crowned with the conversion of many thousand souls! Let not, therefore, such who have fallen by their iniquities but yet return again by sincere repentance say that all their days shall end in darkness, that their names shall ever be unsavory, that they shall always be as barren and dry trees; but let them remember that comfortable promise that God made to repenting Israel, who tells them that He will "get them praise and fame in every land where they have been put to shame" (Zeph. 3:19).

CHAPTER 14

Promises for Future Ages

The third query which I shall propound and endeavor to satisfy is what use a believer may make of all those glorious and rich promises which he can never expect to see the performance of, such as are the beauty and prosperity of the church in peace and holiness, when all pricking briers and grieving thorns shall be removed out of the midst of it: the calling and conversion of the Jews, the downfall and ruin of Antichrist, all which seem to be as blessings reserved for future ages and not to be hoped for in the present times.

To this I answer that true it is that the promises of God are as bonds of a different date, and successively take place in several ages and generations of the church, being so purposely ordered by the infinite wisdom of God, that though He be continually accomplishing some one or other of His blessed promises unto His people, there might yet be a most plentiful reserve of new mercies unto the last ages of the world, that so it might appear that former generations have not exhausted or diminished the treasure of His love and bounty to the prejudice of those that should succeed them. But yet such promises which future times and not the present shall see to be fulfilled, are of much use unto present believers and by the due application of them may yield much satisfaction and comfort unto those who like the patriarchs can see them afar off, and being persuaded of the truth of them do joyfully embrace them as mariners do the desired port at a distance (Heb. 11:13). It was a great comfort and contentment unto Moses that though God would not let him enter into the land of promise, yet before his death He would from the top of Pisgah give him a full prospect of its glory and beauty (Deut. 34:1). And so to a believer it must needs be a matter of much joy and delight that though he cannot live to partake of the future mercies that God has reserved for His church, yet he may by the eye of faith have a distinct view of them in the promises, as in a lively map, and may behold the glory of that portion of blessing and goodness which God will bestow upon His people in the ages that are to come. But more particularly there may be a fourfold use made by a believer of all such promises, whose accomplishment seems to be at a remote distance and period of times.

Support for the Troubled

First, they are useful to support and bear up believers under present troubles and sore afflictions that the church may be exercised with, that it shall not be ruined and undone by them. "The church is as a ship," says Augustine, "which may be tossed with tempests but cannot be sunk and shipwrecked by them."[1] It being the only heir of all the promises that God has made, it must live to enjoy them, else they must become void and of no effect, or be as goods that have no person[2] or Lord to lay claim unto them. And if we consult the Scriptures, we shall find that in the times which were most dark and overcast, God did most frequently use such promises to confirm to His people their deliverance out of present straits, that were not to take

---

1. *Navicula est quae turbari potest, sed mergi non potest.*
2. *bona adespota.*

place till many ages after, that from thence they might conclude their condition not to be hopeless and desperate in regard of future blessings which God would perform to their succeeding generations. Thus, when Jacob was in Egypt, where his seed were oppressed with a long and heavy bondage, he prophesies that the scepter should not depart from Judah till Shiloh came (Gen. 49:10). So when Rezin, king of Syria, and Pekah, king of Israel, joined in a confederacy against Judah, and that the hearts of the people through fear were as the trees of the wood, when moved with the wind (Isa. 7:1–2), the Lord to assure His people that they should be delivered, and that their attempts against Jerusalem should not come to pass, gives no other sign but this: "Behold, a virgin shall conceive, and bear a son, and shall call his name Immanuel" (Isa. 7:14). It was the land in which the Savior of the world was to be born, and they the tribe from which He was to descend. And, therefore, they might be fully confident that for that very promise sake ruin and extirpation should not befall them. So again, in Israel's long captivity of seventy years, though multitudes of them in that long tract of time could expect no other liberty than to be free among the dead, yet the Lord in the beginning of it does by the prophecy of Jeremiah, which was to be read unto them, promise deliverance out of it and comforts them with the assurance of their freedom and their enemies ruin, of both which He makes the casting of the prophet's book into the midst of Euphrates to be a sign unto them (Jer. 51:63–64). And why then may not we in these distracted and divided times, both in regard of opinion and practice, yet hope and believe that those blessed promises of peace and union with which God has promised to beautify His church shall at length be performed; and from thence gather so much present comfort as not to deem our breaches incurable and past all healing? True it is that Christians are like bees gone forth into so many swarms, as that to reason it seems beyond possibility that ever they should by the sound of the word (as by a golden bell) be brought under one hive. But yet that one promise of God's giving His people one heart, and one way, that they may fear Him forever for the good of them and their children after them (Jer. 32:39) is enough to support those that are peacemakers that their labor shall not be in vain, and to comfort those that mourn for the sad rents that are made that there is hope in Israel concerning this thing.

Confident Grounds for Prayer

Secondly, such promises are useful to believers as a firm rock to bottom their prayers upon, which they make on the behalf of the church. To pray that Christ's kingdom may come, and that it may spread itself unto the utmost ends of the earth, is the duty of every Christian. But the ground of their making such prayers, and of their confidence in obtaining them, wholly arises from the promises that God has made. He it is who has promised that Christ shall reign till He has put all His enemies under His feet (1 Cor. 15:25). He it is who has said that Zion shall suck the milk of the Gentiles, and shall suck the breasts of kings (Isa. 60:16). That her horn shall be iron, and her hoofs brass, to break in pieces many people (Mic. 4:13). And thereby are they encouraged to seek His face and to put Him in mind of His gracious promises unto His people. True it is that the times and seasons when these things shall be are unknown unto them, neither are they to be curious and anxious about them, God having put them in His own power (Acts 1:7). But yet knowing that He who has promised is faithful, they do with delight plead them in their prayers, and with faith embrace them in their arms.

Evidence of Sincere Love

Thirdly, such promises are useful to try the sincerity of a believer's affection and love to God's glory, and to the welfare of the church. Promises wherein men's present interests are concerned, self-love may make them to put a value upon them, and quicken an ardency both in their prayers and desires to beg the performance of them, as judging themselves to be most happy in the enjoyment of those blessings which are held forth in them. And surely from this very principle are many stirred up to plead with much earnestness the promises of protection when they are under some imminent danger; the promises of provision, when under some pinching want; the promises of comfort, when under some sore affliction. But when a Christian can rejoice in such promises, which speak the future happiness of the church when he is dead and gone, when it is sweet to him to think that Christ's throne shall hereafter be more exalted, His name more known, His Spirit more plentifully poured forth, that the church shall triumph over its enemies, and be a habitation of peace, [and] of love, it is an argument of a noble frame of heart, and of a spirit that is truly affected with the love of God's glory. When a man can ruminate upon such promises with delight, and can in prayer manifest that it is the desire of his soul that these things, wherein God will be so highly honored, may be effected, it is a comfortable evidence that the white at which he levels,[3] and the end which he propounds to himself, does not terminate in his private interest but in the exaltation of the name of God, which by faith he is persuaded shall be magnified throughout all ages of the world.

Comfort Regarding Posterity

Fourthly, such promises are useful to comfort believers in regard of their posterity. It is ofttimes a perplexing thought to tender parents, especially in difficult times, to think what will become

---

3. An allusion to an archer's target.

of their children if they should be taken from them, and their seed be deprived of the benefit of that care and counsel, which while they live they constantly partake of. And this very thing begets as much anxiety in their hearts as the departure of Christ did in His disciples, it being an evil that though foreseen they scarce know how satisfactorily to provide against. Now besides those general considerations drawn from those compassions and bowels that are in God, and His faithfulness in providing for the righteous and their seed according to His promise, all which may help to allay such distrustful thoughts and cares, there may also not a little support and comfort be taken from the exercising of faith on such eminent promises as declare the riches of God's goodness to the ages and times that are to come. All which God will according to their appointed seasons fulfill until that grand and last promise of gathering all His elect unto Himself in glory be accomplished. So that believers may comfortably hope that what promises they fall short of, their posterity shall in one kind or other be partakers of. And though through the dark dispensations of present providences, the church may seem to be in the midst of a howling wilderness, rather than near the borders of a Canaan, yet surely the land of rest is not afar off, though it may to us be out of sight.

CHAPTER 15

Comfort of Assurance in Death

The fourth query is whether believers who are most diligent in the daily application of the promises and in the use of all means to make their calling and election sure always enjoy the comfort of assurance in death, or have, as the apostle expressed it, an entrance abundantly ministered unto them into the everlasting kingdom of our Lord and Savior Jesus Christ (2 Peter 1:11). The answer that I shall give unto this question will consist of divers branches, which I shall lay down in four propositions.

Struggles Often Worse at Death

The first is that a believer as he meets with many brunts and conflicts in his life, so he may and often does meet with worse at his death. Christ's agony and sufferings were sharpest towards the close and end of His life. And then, though He complains not of God, yet in a most vehement expostulation He complains to God, "My God, my God, why hast thou forsaken me?" (Matt. 27:46). Lamb-like and silent deaths are not always the portion of God's dearest children. The wicked may have no pains and bands in their death (Ps. 73:4), when the best of saints may be environed with terrors. The one may be as a man in a sleep who may have pleasant and golden dreams, and the other as a man awake that is afflicted and disquieted with grievous and sore paroxysms.[1] Thus, good Hezekiah, in that sickness in which he was by the prophet summoned to prepare for death, through the sad apprehensions of God's displeasure, poured forth his soul in bitter complaints, "I reckoned till morning, that, as a lion, so will he break all my bones" (Isa. 38:13). And, verse 14, "Like a crane or a swallow, so did I chatter." Grief and pain had both so filled and wasted him that he could only make an indistinct and confused noise, as those birds do when they are deprived of their young ones. And, therefore, Christians are not to be discouraged as if some new thing had befallen them, if in the close and shutting up of their lives, instead of comfortable gales and breathings of the Spirit, they find (contrary to their expectation) Satan to assault them, or God to withdraw Himself from them, who, for a moment, hides His face but with everlasting kindness will embrace them (Isa. 54:8).

Diligence Required

The second proposition is that our diligence to clear up our interest in the promises, and the using of all means to make our calling and election sure, is the ordinary and regular way to obtain comfort, and enlargement in death. To expect to die comfortably, and not to live holily, is as vain as for a man to look for stars on earth and trees in heaven. To waste the oil of grace, and yet to think to be anointed with the oil of gladness, is the fruit of presumption and not of faith. When servants idle out the light that their masters give them to work by, they may well conclude that they must go to bed in the dark. And so when Christians neglect in the day of their life to work out their salvation with fear and trembling, it is no wonder if in the night of death they want the light of comfort, and have a dark exit out of the world.

---

1. *paroxysm*: an episode of increased severity of illness.

Exceptional Cases

The third proposition is that the improvement of the promises, and the diligent use of all means to make our calling and election sure, is not only the ordinary and regular way, but usually procures comfort in death, unless it be in four particular cases.

Sever Sickness

First, when sicknesses and distempers are violent, so as to interrupt and suspend the use of reason, it must needs be that thereby also the comforts of grace be so far eclipsed as to be like stars in a cloudy night, which though they be not blotted out of their orb, yet do not shine. Who can expect that an untuned instrument should ever make a melodious harmony? No more can any man rationally conceive that when the frame of nature is out of order, and the organs of the body wholly indisposed to the acts of reason, that then the comforts of the Spirit should appear in their beauty and luster? Now that God ofttimes puts a period unto the lives of His dearest children by such diseases cannot be denied, for Solomon tells us that all things come alike unto all; there is one event to the righteous, and to the wicked; to the good and to the clean, and to the unclean; to him that sacrifices, and to him that sacrifices not (Eccl. 9:2).

Vehement Temptations

Secondly, when temptations and assaults from Satan are like vehement winds which shake the tree, though they do not overturn it. A man who has a fair estate of lands may by vexatious suites be so put to try his title that he may take little pleasure in the revenues and profits issuing from them; and so a believer in his combating and wrestling with temptations may so far be disquieted that though he question not his condition, he may yet enjoy less satisfaction and present delight in his evidences and assurance than formerly he had. Thus Paul, after his rapture into the third heaven (2 Cor. 12:2), was buffeted by a messenger of Satan, whereby he was not only kept from being exalted above measure, but also interrupted in the enjoyment of those choice comforts and contemplations which such revelations might minister unto him, as may appear by his frequency and importunity in prayer to God to be delivered from this sad conflict [in] verse 8.

Spiritual Negligence

Thirdly, when Christians have intermitted that wonted care and circumspection to preserve their peace and communion with God which formerly they used. When they have been more forgetful of God, and less delighted with His presence than before they were. When they have suffered the world to steal away their thoughts, and affections from heaven, and through a distempered appetite relish more their daily bread than the spiritual manna. When they grow regardless of Christ's voice and open not their hearts to Him who seeks and entreats an admittance, then it is no wonder if their sun set in a cloud and that the horror of a sad darkness takes hold upon them; that then like the spouse in the Canticles they complain that their Beloved has withdrawn Himself and is gone; that they seek Him but cannot find Him; that they call Him by all His blessed and gracious names, and yet He answers not (Song 5:6).

Divine Lessons

Fourthly, when their graces and also their comforts have been already fully manifested, both to themselves and others, in the time of their life, God may in the approaches of death, for sundry reasons best known unto Himself, withdraw His comfortable presence and not fill their souls with those exultations of joy and peace which others might expect to be mingled with their last agonies and expirations in death, so that they should be carried up to heaven in the light of a glorious plerophory[2] like to the angel which ascended in the flame of Manoah's sacrifice (Judg. 13:20). God may do it:

1. To try and manifest the strength of their faith, that though their feelings are not strong, yet their faith is not weak; that though they see not the crown of bliss and immortality hovering as it were over them, and ready to fall upon their heads, they yet believe that it is laid up for them, and that they shall ere long see it and enjoy it together. Such faith highly glorifies God, and in some respects gives more honor unto Him than assurance, which has a kind of sense joined with it, that, like Thomas, sees and believes. But this sees not and yet believes that what God has promised He will perform.

2. God may do it that others may learn that comforts and manifestations of love in death are not so necessary as grace, and therefore not to be dismayed and dejected in their thoughts concerning themselves, if they find not such overflowings of joy and prelibations[3] of heaven itself as some others have had in the time of death. All believers, though they are heirs of the same kingdom, yet have not the same abundant entrance ministered unto them. To some, the passage is like the going upon a clear and crystal stream, which has flowery and aromatical banks on each side of it; to others, it is like a calm and quiet sea on which as the fluctuations and tossings are few or none, so the gales that carry them to the port are not strong and quick. As their temptations are not great, so neither are their comforts glorious.

3. God may do it in judgment to others; that such who have known and seen the light of holiness shining in their lives, and yet have not in the least been advantaged by it should not get the least good by their deaths. As they have not profited by their

---

2. *plerophory*: full assurance.
3. *prelibation*: foretaste.

graces, so neither will He let them be edified by their comforts. Carnal men are ofttimes more ready to observe the dying of holy persons than their lives, because then they conceive it may be seen what reality there is in that profession which they have made of having communion with God and of enjoying His peculiar presence in a differing manner from the world. Now they think it will appear whether their faith be anything beyond a fancy; whether their joys be such as death will not cast a damp upon, as well as upon the delights and pleasures of the world. And when their curiosity is unsatisfied in what they expected, then they spare not to censure them as deceivers both of themselves, and others. Little considering that the just ground of God's causing such bright stars to set in a cloud may be to hide from them what might benefit them in their death, who have learned nothing from the holy example of their lives. The obstinate Jews opposed the doctrine which Christ taught, and rejected the salvation which He offered unto them while He was among them. And then, at His death, [they] insultingly asked for miracles that might declare Him to be the Son of God, whereby they might believe on Him (Matt. 27:42). But God then made His death a stone of stumbling for them to fall at, who had made His life and converse among them to be the object of scorn both to themselves and others.

Life Better Evidence Than Death

The fourth proposition is that the judgment and estimate which believers and others make concerning men's spiritual estates and conditions should chiefly be grounded upon their lives rather than their deaths. There may many accidents fall out in their death, which as they do not prejudice a believer's salvation, so neither should they his Christian reputation. He may through a fever become phrenetical;[4] through melancholy, he may be lumpish and heavy; through temptations, he may be unsettled; through desertions, he may speak uncomfortable speeches and be afflicted with despairing thoughts. His darkness may be without the least glimmerings of light; his agonies in death without sense of comfort. And yet he may be a dear child of God, because, as holy Greenham says,[5] we shall not be judged according to that particular instant of death but according to the general course of our life; not according to our deeds in that present but according to the desires of our hearts ever before. And, therefore, we are not to mistrust God's mercy in death, be it never so uncomfortable, if so be it has been before sealed in our vocation and sanctification. It is sad indeed when the lives and days of those do in such a manner determine and expire who have wasted their time and strength in sinful exorbitances, and have been eaten up with the cares and thoughts of the world, without the least minding of their eternal condition, till arrested by the stroke of death and summoned to appear at the tribunal of a provoked God. But else, though the close of a holy life be most uncomfortable, and full of darkness, it is no just ground to any to change their apprehension and persuasion concerning the welfare of their everlasting estate, having beforehand seen and known such unblameableness of conversation, [and] such fruits of grace, as might clearly evidence the uprightness and sincerity of their hearts towards God and men.

---

4. *phrenetical*: frenzied.

5. Richard Greenham (ca. 1535–1594), Elizabethan Puritan and promoter of practical piety. Greenham's works were widely read and disseminated; he was heavily influential in the direction of the early Puritan movement and wrote a popular treatise on the Sabbath.

CHAPTER 16

Use of Temporal Promises

The fifth and last query that I shall propound is what use is to be made of temporal promises, such wherein preservation from outward evils, the free and liberal donation of earthly blessings, the removal of sad and heavy pressures, are in particular promised and undertaken for by God in His Word. After what manner are believers to act and exercise their faith upon them, or to hope for the performance of them; in regard that they ofttimes who may best plead their title and interest in them do most of all want the fruition of such mercies. "They," says the apostle, of whom the world was not worthy, "wandered about in sheepskins and goatskins; being destitute, afflicted, tormented" (Heb. 11:37).

The answer to this question, I do not purpose to make as the cords of a tent stretched out to their utmost length, or unnecessarily to enlarge as the Pharisees did with affectation their phylacteries; but yet for the more full and just solution of it, I conceive it will not be impertinent to speak to three particulars. First, to show why God under the Old Testament did make the tenor of His promises to run so universally of His giving unto them the blessings and enjoyments of this life, when as under the gospel such kind of promises are more sparingly recorded, and not so distinctly set down. Secondly, to show the various advantage and profit that believers may reap to their spiritual estate by looking unto such promises with an eye of faith, and quietly waiting the good pleasure of God for the fulfilling of them. Thirdly, to give rules for the right understanding of the nature of temporal promises, and the manner of due applying them unto our particular exigencies and conditions.

Promises of Temporal Mercies under the Law

For the first, that is, God's making unto His people so many distinct and redoubled promises of temporal mercies, sundry reasons might be assigned, but I shall fix only upon this: that such a way of bounty was most suitable to the winning of their observance unto such administrations and forms of worship as He then gave them in command, and required their obedience unto. For "until the time of reformation [came]," as the apostle expresses it (Heb. 9:10); that is, until the time of the New Testament, when both the imperfection of the law and priesthood was to be done away by Christ, who, as a more excellent Priest offered up a most perfect sacrifice, all things were transacted after an earthly and external manner. The sanctuary was worldly (Heb. 9:1). The ordinances imposed on them were carnal, which stood in meats, and drinks, and divers washings (Heb. 9:10). Now to this pedagogy of the church, the promises of such outward blessings were most agreeable. The duties and exercises of their religion were most conversant about the outward man; so likewise the promises that were the encouragements to move and incite them to an observance of those prescribed rites were such as did chiefly hold forth the prosperity and welfare of their outward estate. Not that the goodness of God to His people, or His covenant with them, did extend only to the care of their bodies, or that this was the utmost drift of those many promises which He had made unto them. This had been, as Peter Martyr[1] speaks, to have made God to have had no more regard to His church than shepherds have to their flock, or herdsmen to their cattle, who look no further than to their thriving and well-liking in their pastures. But as in their sacrifices, and other ceremonies of their worship they were trained up and instructed in the knowledge of spiritual duties towards God in which their hearts and thoughts were to be employed. So also by the temporal promises were grounds laid of carrying on their faith and hope for the obtaining of more glorious mercies than those which at the present they enjoyed. Their manna was a kind of sacramental food, and the water from the rock a sacramental drink, the land of Canaan a type of the true and heavenly rest, which Christ has purchased, which by Him who was the substance of all shadows they might expect. True it is that both the precepts of their worship and the promises of their reward were more dark and obscure than the rule of our obedience, and the recompense of our service under the gospel, but yet both did center and terminate in one and the same end. The state of the church under the law was represented, says Brightman,[2] by a "sea of brass,"[3] which is of a more thick and dark substance, but under the gospel by "a sea of glass" (Rev. 4:6),[4] which is most clear and transparent.

Benefits of Temporal Promises

The second particular is to show the several benefits that redound to believers by looking unto temporal promises with an eye of

---

1. Peter Martyr Vermigli (1499–1562), Italian Reformer, author of several notable works on the Lord's Supper.

2. Thomas Brightman (1562–1607), English clergyman, biblical commentator, and author of an influential commentary on the book of Revelation.

3. *mare aereum.*

4. *mare vitreum.*

faith. And here many might be insisted on, but I shall insist only on four.

Mortifies Inordinate Desires
First, faith in the promises of this life much helps to the mortification of inordinate desires and of distracting and anxious cares, both which are the genuine fruits and offspring of unbelief. Every man is conscious unto himself both of his own wants and of the fading condition of every creature, and thereby he is stirred up to seek in a restless manner a supply of present necessities and a solicitous provision for all future contingencies. Ask many a man why he toils so incessantly to the breaking of his head with cares and his body with labor, and he will quickly tell you that he has none to trust unto but himself, that he knows not what hard times and changes may come. Sickness may befall him, and waste what he has gotten; age may overtake him, and render him unapt for labor; charges may multiply in his family, and it is not the air that will feed them. He had need, therefore, to do what he does. If not, he and his might starve. But now when a believer can look unto the promise, how soon are all these tempestuous thoughts and fears calmed? How sweetly is the heart quieted by casting all its care upon God, who cares for us (1 Peter 5:7)? How quickly can he spy in the promises God's obligation for clothing to cover his nakedness, for meat to satisfy his hunger, for physic to cure his diseases, for armor to safeguard his person, for treasure to provide for his family and posterity? How fully can he rest contented in the things which he has, because God has said, "I will never leave thee, nor forsake thee" (Heb. 13:5).

Strengthens Faith
Secondly, faith exercised on the temporal promises will much help to strengthen our adherence to the promises of a better life and cause us to trust more perfectly in God for the salvation

of our souls. Our Savior tells His disciples that if God fed the fowls, and clothed the lilies, He will much more provide for them which are better than they (Matt. 6:26). And so may a believer argue with himself [that] if God has made so many rich promises of provision for the body, He will not be wanting to the happiness of the soul. If He be so careful of the casket, He will not be unmindful of the jewel. If He give daily bread to the one, He will surely give manna to the other. If He make our pilgrimage delightful, and make the paths of our feet to drop fatness, He will make our rest and habitation with Himself to be glorious. If the feet tread on roses here, and on the moon and stars hereafter, how orient and beautiful will be that crown of life that shall be set upon our heads? Such kinds of argumentation are very helpful to a believer, who owns all his outward comforts to arise from God's faithfulness in His promise, though in the mere and naked having of them "no man knoweth either love or hatred" (Eccl. 9:1).

Sweetens Blessings

Thirdly, faith exercised on the promises of this life sweetens the enjoyment of every blessing, be it little or much. There are two sources from whence all outward mercies flow, the providence of God and the promise of God: the one is as the nether springs from which every creature receives its preservation and continuance. He opens His hand, and satisfies the desire of every living thing (Ps. 145:16). The other is as the upper springs from which after a peculiar manner the goodness and bounty of God is conveyed unto believers. Godliness has the "promise of the life that now is, and of that which is to come" (1 Tim. 4:8). Now the streams that flow from this fountain are more pure, and free from that vexation and vanity which the abundance that the wicked has is subject unto, because they are sanctified by Christ, in whom all the promises are yea and amen. When, therefore, a believer can look upon all his outward enjoyments as the fruits of God's special love, and can say as Jacob did, [that] these are the blessings which God has graciously given His servant (Gen. 33:5), then they become in their use more delightful, and in their taste more sweet. A small portion of meat given by the hand of a great personage is more set by and esteemed than all the variety of his full table upon which his other guests feed and carve themselves, because it carries with it a particular character and mark of favor to him on whom it is bestowed. And so a little given by God as a testimony of His peculiar love and care towards believers is more desirable and satisfactory than great revenues that flow only from a common bounty.

Preserves from Unlawful Means

Fourthly, faith exercised on the temporal promises is a powerful antidote to preserve believers from the use of unlawful means, both in the seeking and in the obtaining of all earthly comforts. The inordinacy of the desires puts men ofttimes upon dangerous precipices: "He that maketh haste to be rich shall not be innocent" (Prov. 28:20). So, "They that will be rich fall into temptation and a snare, and into many foolish and hurtful lusts" (1 Tim. 6:9). Now faith, though it does not take off the edge of men's industry and diligence in the pursuance of all lawful and just means, or make them to expect to be fed as the fowls of the air that neither sow nor reap, or to be clothed as the lilies of the field that neither spin nor labor, yet it does so correct and allay the vehemency of all desires towards the things of this world, as that they dare not take any way to gain them, which the Word does not warrant, or the promise sanctify. Faith suggests to them that it is not their labor and care that makes rich but God's blessing, who gives no sorrow with it (Prov. 10:22); that it is not their wisdom that makes their endeavors in their calling to be successful, but God's fidelity and truth that crowns them with prosperity; that it is not their sweat that feeds the lamp of their comforts and makes it to shine but the constant droppings and distillations of God's goodness. And thereby they are enabled to depend upon His promise, and to believe that such a dimensum,[5] and portion of outward blessings shall be given unto them, as that they may truly say with the prophet, "The lines are fallen unto me in pleasant places; yea, I have a goodly heritage" (Ps. 16:6).

The Right Understanding of Temporal Promises

The third particular is the giving of rules for the right understanding of the nature of temporal promises, and the manner of due applying them unto ourselves, which I shall set down in these five subsequent assertions.

Expedient Limitations

First, that God's declaration in His promises of giving temporal blessings is not absolute but carries with it a tacit condition and limitation of expediency. The great and utmost end of all the promises is one and the same with that which is the chief end of man, the fruition of God, and communion with Him in everlasting blessedness. Now the means that are subservient to this end are either such as are of absolute necessity, and do immediately prepare and dispose the soul for the obtaining of it, or else such as are less requisite and have only a remote and consequential tendency thereunto; and that not of themselves but as they are overruled by God, who makes all things to work together for good[6] to them that love him [Rom. 8:28]. And of this kind are all temporal blessings, prosperity, riches, health, freedom, and the like. All which do, as I conceive, come no further under the verge of a promise than as they conduce to the happiness of the other

---

5. *dimensum*: a measured portion, fixed allowance.

6. *omnia cooperari in bonum.*

life, this life being only a way and passage unto it, as the wilderness was to Israel to bring them to Canaan. Because, therefore, none can know what is that measure of these outward comforts, which most tends to the furtherance of their eternal happiness, which in and above all things ought to be eyed by them, it being haply more for their spiritual good to have many advantages of this life in a less degree rather than in a greater, to want them rather than to enjoy them. They cannot, then, in their supplications to God, seek the absolute performance of His promises in temporal blessings but must refer themselves to His wisdom and faithfulness so to order and measure out the comforts of this life unto them, as may best stand with the welfare of their everlasting condition, without which all earthly happiness is no other than a splendid misery. But it is much otherwise in the blessings of grace and holiness, which are things so essential to a believer's fruition of God as that without faith he cannot please God (Heb. 11:6); without holiness, he cannot see God (Heb. 12:14); without being born of water, and of the Spirit, he cannot enter into the kingdom of God (John 3:3). And being, therefore, so intrinsically good in themselves, so absolutely also necessary unto salvation, they are in prayer to be most absolutely sought, as considered in their essence. But their degrees are arbitrary: God giving to some a less, [and] to others a greater measure of grace, according to His pleasure.

Disjunctive Fulfillment

The second assertion is that the fulfilling of temporal promises is disjunctive, God either giving the blessing itself, or that which is equivalent unto it. The promises of God are all made in Christ, and derive their certainty and stability from Him in whom they are made, not from us to whom they are made. They are all ratified with the same oath, and purchased by the same blood. And though they are not equally precious in regard of the things promised, yet they are equally true in regard of the certainty of their performance, only the manner of their fulfilling is different. In the spiritual promises, God gives the things in kind; for how can they be otherwise made good? What is answerable in worth or excellency to grace, the least drop of which is of more value than the whole creation. In temporals, God gives the things themselves, or makes a compensation some other way. If riches be asked of Him in prayer, and yet denied, He makes it up in contentation,[7] which brings that satisfaction with it that riches cannot yield. If health be prayed for, and not granted, He gives strength to bear the cross by putting under His everlasting arms. If deliverance in trouble be desired, and not obtained, He gives the divine consolations of martyrs, which that noble Landgrave of Hessia[8] said he found in his long and tedious imprisonment. And in thus doing, God does not break His promise, but changes it to the better. It is said of our Savior that, "in the days of his flesh, when he had offered up prayers and supplications with strong crying and tears unto him that was able to save him from death, and was heard in that he feared" (Heb. 5:7). That which Christ prayed for was deliverance: "O my Father, if it be possible, let this cup pass from me" (Matt. 26:39). Was there then any defect in Christ's faith, in that He did not obtain the thing prayed for? Or how was His prayer heard? Did He not die the death of the cross? Was He not buried in the grave? Yes, but yet He had from God an answer of supportation,[9] though not of deliverance. He was strengthened in His agony by the appearance of an angel (Luke 22:43). He was assured by God's promise of victory over death, though not of freedom from it.

---

7. *contentation*: being made content.

8. Maurice, Landgrave of Hesse-Kassel (1572–1632), German Lutheran convert to Calvinism.

9. *supportation*: being supported.

He underwent the darkness of the grave, but not the corruption of it (Ps. 16:10).

Redemptive Qualification

The third assertion is that temporal promises are to be expounded with the reservation and exception of the cross. God, in the covenant of grace, which is the adequate measure of His obligation to believers, has kept to Himself this prerogative of chastening the delinquencies of His children with rods (Ps. 89:32–33), of withdrawing His favors from them when they withhold their obedience to Him, of exercising the severity of a Father, as well as the indulgence of a Mother. And, therefore, believers, when they want the staff of many outward comforts in their hand, and feel the smart of the rod of affliction upon their back, they are not to suspect God's fidelity in His promise but to reflect upon themselves, and by a serious disquisition, to consider from whence the suspension of any good things that He has promised arises. And if Christians under God's rebukes did make this their chief task, they would be so far from charging Him with unfaithfulness, as that they would more wonder that God is pleased to vouchsafe them anything that are prodigals that justly deserve nothing. In the midst of their deepest trials, they would say as the church did in her extremities, "It is of the LORD's mercies that we are not consumed…great is thy faithfulness" (Lam. 3:22–23).

Prayerful Reception

The fourth assertion is that temporal mercies in the promises are only to be obtained by a well-regulated prayer, in which God is sought after a right manner and the mercies begged for a right end.

1. The manner of seeking God must be in faith, "Let him ask in faith, nothing wavering" (James 1:6). But the faith here required is not the faith of a particular persuasion that God will

give the very thing itself that we beg of Him but the faith of submission, by which we resolve our prayers into His will and believe that He will do whatever is best for our good and His glory. We then distrust God when either we are jealous of His willingness to perform His word, or of His power to accomplish His word. But when we acknowledge the all-sufficiency of His power, and resign our desires to His will, we do then pray in faith. And this was the faith that our Lord Christ did put forth in His prayer, when He said, "Not my will, but thine, be done" (Luke 22:42). I do not deny but that God may sometimes assure and incline the hearts of His children that are importunate wrestlers in prayer to be confident of granting the temporal blessing that they seek, but this is a confidence that is rather begotten by the Spirit in the height and vigor of prayer than brought with us unto the duty. Sometimes, I say, such a confidence may be, but it is neither ordinary nor usual.

2. Temporal mercies must be asked for a right end, "Ye ask, and receive not, because ye ask amiss; that ye may consume it upon your lusts" (James 4:3). Carnal lusts may make men eager in prayer but not successful. Usually, wrong ends in prayer are accompanied with disappointments. Sinister aims turn duties of worship into acts of self-seeking; they change the voice of prayer into a brutish howling (Hos. 7:14); the execution of justice itself into murder (Hos. 1:4); the end in moral things is the same that the form is in natural things.[10] The quality and goodness of them is not discerned but by the end. It concerns, therefore, believers that would in prayer obtain any outward blessing to look unto their ends in asking of it; though the mercy be earthly, yet their end in asking of it must be heavenly. God's glory must be in the end of all prayer, as His name must be in the beginning of it,

---

10. *finis in moralibus idem est, quod forma in naturalibus.*

else it cannot be expected that it should be owned as a sacrifice by him.

Secondary Expectation

The fifth assertion is that the blessings of temporal promises are to be sought secondarily, and not primarily (Matt. 6:33). They are neither to be the chief cares of our life, or desires of our prayers, because the soul may do well without the body, but the body cannot do well without the soul. And yet of this disorder the greatest part of men may be found guilty. Their estates they carefully put into their deeds and evidences, and their souls they only put into their wills, the last of instruments that are usually either made or sealed. For the one they think it enough, if, with a few gilded expressions of piety, it be given and bequeathed as a legacy unto God. But for the other they conceive no paints or toil too great to increase it, or cost too much for to secure it. The one they make the task of the morning and day of their lives, the other the by-work of the evening and the approaching night of death. So that it is no wonder, if, in these preposterous and irregular actings of men, they do not find the blessing of God's promise upon their labors that they toil as in the fire, and weary themselves for very vanity (Hab. 2:13); that they sow much, and bring in little (Hag. 1:6). For what benefit can they justly expect to reap from the promise who neglect to walk by the guidance of that rule to which the promise is made?

CHAPTER 17

The Neglect or Abuse of the Promises

Having spoken enough (if not too much) to each of those four heads that in the beginning were propounded, and laid as so many cornerstones for this small structure to stand upon, the last head which now remains to be insisted on is the handling of such useful applications and inferences as naturally flow and arise from this doctrinal truth of the transcendent worth and preciousness of the promises which are given unto us by Jesus Christ.

And the first application which I shall make is [that] a sad and just complaint (which sighs and tears may better express than words) of the great injury and contempt that is done unto the blessed promises, both by men's careless and overly seeking after them as things of no great worth, and their sinful perverting of them unto wrong ends and purposes while they turn grace into wantonnesses and sin the more freely because of the redundancy of divine mercy which is manifested in them. God lays it as a heavy charge against Israel that He had written unto them the great things of His law, but they were counted as a strange thing (Hos. 8:12). How much more are they blameworthy who are guilty of despising the *Magnalia Evangelii*, and of setting light by the most choice and excellent things of the gospel, as if they were of little or no importance for the obtaining of life and salvation. This complaint if it had no circumstances to aggravate it, but were only laid in the general against men, that they have forsaken the fountain of living water, and hewed them out cisterns, broken cisterns that can hold no water (Jer. 2:13). It would quickly prove to be so black an indictment, as could neither admit of an excuse to lessen the sin, nor yet of pity to mitigate the punishment that deserves to be inflicted upon such offenders. But if we shall consider it in the several aggravations which heighten it, we may then at this sin justly cry out, "Be astonished, O ye heavens, at this, and be afraid, be ye very desolate." There are five particulars that make the complaint more sad, and the injury which is done unto the promises the more exceeding sinful.

Many Neglect the Promises

The first aggravation is taken from the universality of this sin: they who are transgressors in this matter are not a few. Parisiensis, speaking of David's Psalms, cries out, "Oh! how many dullards has holy David, or rather the Holy Spirit, to His harp, who are little affected with the heavenly melody that it makes?"[1] And may it not be as truly said concerning the precious promises of Christ, Oh! how many are there that taste little or nothing of their sweetness? What vast numbers of men are there who see no more worth and beauty in them than blind persons do in the sun? How many be there that spend and blaze away the lamp of their time in frothy studies and curious speculations but seldom or never look into the Bible to read and understand what their interest right is to the blessings of heaven by the promises? How ambitious are others to be thought to know much of the mind of God concerning His decrees, which are as a sealed book but

---

1. *Eheu! Quot* ὄνους *habet sanctus David, vel potiùs Spiritus sanctus ad suam Cytharam.*

neglect to see and know both His will and love in the gospel and the promises, which are as a book wide open, written in fair and legible characters for all to look into? In the one their travel and labor is fruitless like that of the ants, which often climb high trees to seek for food, but when they are at the top return empty, not being able to bring any thing down with them. But in the other it would prove like that of the bee, which seeks its aliment among fragrant flowers, and fails not to return to its hive laden with honey. O! that ministers who seem to converse with the promises more than others were not guilty of this great sin while they only read and study them as lawyers do other men's evidences and titles of land, without any respects of being proprietaries themselves. Or else are, as Bernard expresses it, like the teeth which chew meat for the whole body but derive so sweetness from it that may delight or profit them.[2] Oh! that many who look upon themselves as true heirs of the promises were not injurious to the worth and dignity of them, while they make the success of providences the warrant of the goodness of their actions, rather than the stability of the promises, which in all undertakings are the surest guides for to direct and the best comforters for to encourage. It is the observation of Sulpicius[3] concerning the ancient Jews that always in prosperity, being unmindful of heavenly blessings, they worshipped idols, and in their adversity the true God.[4] And so it may be said concerning many professors in these present times that in external successes and prosperous events, they altogether adore and extoll providences; but when these frown upon them, or grow cloudy, then they betake themselves to promises.

---

2. *qui toti corpori masticant cibum, et nullum inde saporem habent.*

3. Sulpicius Severus (ca. 363–ca. 425), early Christian writer, historian, and biographer. He is best known for writing the life of St. Martin.

4. *Semper in secundis rebus immemores coelestium beneficiorum, idolis supplicabant, in adversis Deo.*

The Vanity of Earthy Things

A second aggravation is from the vanity and emptiness of those things which men set their hearts upon. The mind of man is the supreme and most noble faculty of the soul, indued by God with such abilities and graces which abundantly declare that earthly things can no more satisfy it, or fill it, than the breath of the mariners can fill the sails. And, therefore, God has provided for it suitable objects on which it may exercise both its natural power, and the supernatural habits, which by His Spirit He infuses into it with fullness of delight and satisfaction. He has, in His Word, revealed high mysteries which the glorious angels desire to pry into (1 Peter 1:12), in the contemplation of which the mind of believers may be ever fruitfully busied. And He has also made precious promises both of grace and glory, on which their faith may certainly rest, and from which it may derive more sweetness and contentment in one hour than the fruition of all earthly perfections will ever be able to yield in a succession of ages. And yet how apt are believers as well as others to let their thoughts to fix and dwell on these empty things that are below, rather than to study and delight themselves in the knowledge [of] these divine and angelical objects? How often do they more resemble in their conversation the Israelites that were scattered abroad throughout the land of Egypt to gather straw and stubble (Ex. 5:12), than the wise merchant that spent his time in seeking goodly pearls (Matt. 13:45). And do they not by such preposterous and irregular actings greatly undervalue, and highly dishonor, the precious things of the gospel? Do they not by thus walking make themselves inhabitants of the world, rather than pilgrims and strangers that seek and desire a heavenly country? Oh! therefore, let me prevail with you who believe that God has provided better things for you than others to be exceeding circumspect and cautious, that you let nothing lie nearer your hearts, or take up more of your thoughts, than the promises of life and glory, the expectation of which yields at present the best comfort, and their fruition the most absolute and perfect happiness.

The Mutability of Earthly Things

A third aggravation is from the mutability and uncertainty of all those things which take off the most men both from seeking after the promises and from valuing of them according to their worth. It is a true position of Lessius,[5] in his divine perfections,[6] that duration and aeviternity[7] make a good infinitely better, and an evil infinitely worse.[8] And in this respect the good things which are held forth in the promises far excel all earthly riches or grander whatever, which in their greatest ability are both short and mutable. Can any man say that the wild fowl in his grounds are his which suddenly take their wings and fly away, and for a while make a stay in another man's field, and thereby give a like propriety unto the second, as they did unto the first? No more can any man call riches truly his, which like to winged birds shift their owners and haste from one to another. Have not the present times furnished us with instances in this kind even to astonishment? Have we not seen the glory of nobles stained with ignominy? Have not those that dwelt in stately mansions become as cottagers, and they that sat in low places been invested in stately mansions? Have we not beheld the evil that Solomon complains of, "I have seen servants upon horses, and princes walking as servants upon the earth" (Eccl. 10:7)?

---

5. Leonardus Lessius (1544–1623), Flemish moral theologian, Jesuit, professor at the University of Leuven, and author of *On Justice and Law* (1605), an influential and oft-printed commentary on Aquinas's *Summa Theologica*.

6. *De perfectionibus moribusque divinis* [On the Perfections and Morals of God] (1620).

7. *aeviternity*: everlasting duration, eternity.

8. *aeternitas efficit bonum infinite melius, et malum infinite pejus.*

And yet who is there that by all these changes is awakened to get evidences that will not burn, riches that cannot be plundered, an inheritance that cannot be shaken? Oh! how greedily do men still pursue the fleeting vanities, and neglect the true riches that endure for ever?

Partakers of the Promises

A fourth aggravation is from the facility of being made partakers of the promises. They are precious but not difficult, the terms upon which they are tendered serve rather to invite than to deter. We need not say in our heart, "Who shall ascend into heaven? (that is, to bring Christ down from above:) Or, Who shall descend into the deep? (that is, to bring up Christ again from the dead.) But what saith it? The word is nigh thee" (Rom. 10:6–8). It is no wonder pearls which lie at the bottom of steep rocks have but few adventurers for them, because the danger may be more than the gain, [as] if gold in remote countries and deep mines be not travelled for and dug out of the bowels of the earth. But it may be justly wondered at, and censured as the highest folly, if men coming to a full heap of treasures be invited to throw away the clay and dirt with which their hands are filled, and the superfluities with which they are loaded, and to take of gold and pearl as much as they can carry, should refuse to do the one that they might thereby be enabled to do the other. What is it else that God and Christ require of men to the receiving of the promises, but only that they would disburden themselves of earthly encumbrances, which hinder the reception of spiritual mercies, that so with hearts emptied of worldly affections and cares they may be qualified for the fullness of heavenly riches? When Joseph invited his father and brethren to come down into Egypt, he bids them not to regard their stuff: "for the good of all the land of Egypt is yours" (Gen. 45:20). So the true heavenly Joseph, when He invited men to come unto Him, He bids them not to set their hearts on things on the earth, because all the riches of His kingdom are before them, and by His promises made over to them. How inexcusable then must their neglect be who do not with answerable hearts and desires embrace such precious offers.

The Excellency of the Promises

A fifth aggravation is taken from the command of God and Christ. We are not only invited to take hold of the promises, but we are commanded to believe the excellency of them. This, says the apostle, is His commandment that "we should believe on the name of his Son Jesus Christ" (1 John 3:23). That is, we ought so to believe His promises, His sayings, as to count them worthy of all acceptation. As we assent unto them for their truth, so are we to embrace them for their preciousness and worth. Our faith must work by love; it must put forth itself in the strength of all affection by our esteeming and prizing of them above the most desirable things of the world. Thus David did when he said, "Thy testimonies have I taken as an heritage for ever: for they are the rejoicing of my heart" (Ps. 119:111). God's promises he made as his lands, as his goods, as his all. They were more dear to him than all his temporal things whatsoever. When, therefore, they are not thus honored both in the hearts and in the lives of believers, the great commandment of the gospel is violated, the disobedience of which will be recompensed with more heavy and sore judgments than the breaches of the law.

CHAPTER 18

Differences between the Promises of God and Satan

The second application from this truth that the promises of the gospel are precious shall be to acquaint us with the wide differences that are between the promises of God and the promises of the devil, who is the great deceiver of the whole world (Rev. 12:9). Sin, which Satan by all his arts endeavors to make men guilty of that so they may be as miserable as himself, is in itself so full of deformity and ugliness that if it were but seen in its true shape, there could not be a more effectual argument to keep men from the commission of it than its own monstrosity. There are three things, say the school, that cannot be defined: the amiableness and beauty of God, the informity of the first matter, and the deformity of sin.[1] Now, to hide and cover this misshapen monster, Satan uses not a few devices. Sometimes, he makes it to appear in the habit and likeness of a virtue; and thus he tempts men to covetousness under the notion of frugality, [and] to riot and prodigality under the color of liberality. Sometimes, he varnishes it with the specious shows of profit and gain, and promises large rewards to them that will but comply with his suggestions and counsels. And this is one of the most subtle artifices that he uses to withdraw a man from any good, to entice

---

1. *Dei formositas, materiae primae informitas,* and *peccati deformitas.*

and win him to any sin. Thus, he tempted Balaam to venture upon the cursing of God's people by the promise of honor and preferment; Micah's Levite, with a small augmentation of his stipend promised unto him, he tempted both to theft and idolatry; Judas upon the promise of thirty pieces of silver, which the instruments of the devil make unto him, he tempts to sell the life and blood of his blessed Master, yea, by a frank and large promise of all the kingdoms of the world; he tempts our Lord and Savior to the highest act of idolatry that is imaginable, to fall down and worship him, not despairing by the greatness of the offer to hide the foulness of the sin, though it be with scorn and indignation rejected by Christ (Matt. 4:10). Because, therefore, that the most of men are ready to be deceived by the speciousness of the devil's promises, and to give more heed to what he speaks than to the good Word of God, I shall in four particulars set forth the difference between the promises of God and the promises of Satan.

The Persons That Make Them

The first is the difference between the persons that make them. Promises are like bonds which depend altogether upon the sufficiency of the surety. If a beggar seal to an instrument for the payment of ten thousand pounds, who esteems it to be any better than a blank? But if a man of estate and ability binds himself to pay such a sum, it is looked upon as so much real estate, and men do value themselves by such bills and bonds as well as by what is in their own possession. God, who has made rich promises to believers, is able to perform what He has spoken. He is rich in mercy (Eph. 2:4); abundant in goodness and truth (Ex. 34:6); He is the God of truth (Ps. 31:5); the Father of mercies (2 Cor. 1:3). But the devil is a beggar, an outcast, one that has nothing in possession, nothing in disposition. He is a liar, and the father of it (John 8:44); a deceiver (Rev. 12:9); a murderer from the beginning, who killed not one but all in one (John 8:44). How then can his promises be a foundation of support to any that have no other word to build upon but his? He has never kept his promise, and God has never broke His promise. There has not failed one word of all His good promise, which He promised by the hand of Moses His servant (1 Kings 8:56).

The Matter of the Promises

A second difference is in the matter of the promises. Let us weigh the promises of the one and of the other in the balance of truth, and we shall find that the promises of God are gold, and the promises of the devil are alchemy, such which though they glitter much have no worth or excellency in them. Or, that they are, as Aristotle calls the rainbow, "an appearance only,"[2] and not like the cloud, which he styled "a true and real substance."[3] God's [promises] are substantial realities, and his vanishing and fleeting shadows, windy and swollen bladders, which but a little pricked quickly fall and grow lank. Stobaeus, out of Herodotus, tells a story of one Archetimus, who had deposited money in the hand of Cydias, his friend, who afterwards requiring them again of him, he denied the receiving any. And being thereupon cited before the judges for want of other proof, it was resolved that the matter should be determined by a solemn oath, a day for which being appointed, Cydias feigning illness, provides him a hollow staff into which he put the gold, and while he went to the altar to swear, he gave his staff into the hand of Archetimus to hold, and then swore that he had received money from him, but he had returned them again. Archetimus, being much incensed both by his impudence and his own loss, flings down the staff with such violence upon the ground that it broke into pieces,

---

2. Φάσις.

3. ὑπόσασις.

and the money in it scattered abroad, whereby Cydias's fraud was fully detected. And this the historian calls "a lie made up of art and subtlety."[4] Such are all Satan's promises; they are nothing but well-tempered and fine-spun lies, gilded impostures, cheats framed on purpose to deceive. The matter of them is false, as well as the end of them is deceitful.

The Ground of the Promises

A third difference is in the ground of the promises. God's promises arise from His love and good will to those to whom they are made and are the powerful motives by which He wins and draws men to the obedience of Himself. But Satan's promises flow from his irreconcilable hatred of God, and his envying of man's happiness which God by Christ has freely estated upon him. He cannot bear that God should have any to worship Him, or to love Him, and therefore he uses all ways that malice and envy can prompt unto him to draw and entice men from Him. As God uses His promises to oblige and tie men to Himself as by so many strong cords and bands of love, so Satan on the contrary makes use of his promises to alienate men's hearts and affections from God, and to bring them into bondage to himself. His great end by all these specious artifices of promising honor, riches, pleasure, or whatsoever may be a bait to carnal hearts is at once to deprive God of His glory, and man of his happiness. His promises are as the meat which fowlers set before birds, which is not to feed them but to take them.

The Accomplishment of the Promises

A fourth difference is in the accomplishment. God's promises are always like unto a rich and seasonable harvest, which fully answers the hopes and expectation of the husbandman. They

---

4. τέχνυς πεωλασμένον ψευδὸς.

who wait upon Him have never their faces covered with shame, nor their hearts dejected with disappointments. He is, as Bernard expresses it, "faithful in promising, powerful in performing."[5] God, who cannot lie, has promised (Titus 1:2). But as God is always righteous in keeping His Word, so Satan is always false in breaking his word. If he promise bread, he gives a stone; if fish, a serpent; if riches, poverty. Remigius, who was a judge in Florence, and had many witches under his examination, reports that divers of them have confessed that the seeming gold and money, which they received of him, when it came to be used, proved either leaves or sand, not above the value of three stivers was ever found to be current money. And indeed how can it otherwise be expected? When such is his hatred unto all mankind, as that he continually seeks their ruin and not their welfare? Can any man rationally conceive that he should deal better with him than with our first parents? In propounding the temptation he makes a show of friendship, but in the close he proves a bloody liar. What other thing did they behold by his opening of their eyes but their own shame and folly in hearkening unto his deceitful words? What other knowledge did they gain but only the sad experience of the transitoriness of sinful pleasures, which vanish as soon as they are tasted, and prove to be not food but poison.

Seeing then that in all these respects there is so wide a difference between God's promises, and the devil's, oh, then how inexcusable is their sin who by the enchantments and fascinations of Satan are drawn aside to give more credit unto his bare word than to the promises of God that are ratified with His oath and

---

5. *Verax in promissione, potens in exhibitione.*

Christ's blood! What higher contumely[6] and scorn can any put upon God than by their unbelief to make Him a liar, and that in such a manner to have more regard to what Satan, the father of lies, speaks than to what God, who is the Father of mercies, swears? And yet, in this kind, God suffers dishonor from more than a few. How great is the number of those who upon the appearance of the least difficulty are apt to be jealous of His faithfulness, and through distrust to wave the waiting upon Him in His promise for the obtaining of some particular blessing, and betake themselves unto such ways as Satan secretly suggests to them, to be both more compendious and certain? And what is this less than to be interpretatively guilty, if not formally of so foul a sin as the making of the most holy and righteous God a liar? Let me, therefore, in a few words prevail with all those that profess to the world to have their dependance upon God, and to derive their comforts from His promises, to be circumspect how they comply with any way or means for the effecting of their desires that may be dishonorable to God, and to those most sure promises which He has made of giving them whatsoever they ask of Him according to His will. To speak well, says Isiodorus Pelutiota,[7] is to sound like a cymbal; but to do well is to act like an angel. It is not a believer's work only to speak well of the promises, but to act faith in them; and when through diffidence he steps aside into any unwarrantable path, he then gives occasion unto worldly and carnal men to think and speak as slightly of God's promises as he at other times has spoken unto the world of the deceitfulness and inconstancy of the promises of Satan.

---

6. *contumely*: insulting language, scorn.

7. Isidore of Pelusium (370–449), Desert Father, from a prominent Alexandrian family, known primarily for his letters.

CHAPTER 19

Estates of Believers and Unbelievers

A third application may be this: if the promises that are by Christ are so exceedingly great and precious, then the lowest estate that can befall a believer who has an interest and right unto them is far better than the highest and most glorious condition of any person that can lay no claim or title to them. So that Luther might well say that he would rather be a poor rustic and a Christian than to be great Alexander and a heathen.[1] This corollary, though it be a truth that all contradiction can no more shake than the violence of tempestuous waves can stir the rocks against which they dash and break, yet it has so much of a paradox in it that from the most part of men it may find no better entertainment than Paul's doctrine of the resurrection did at Athens, where he has no better title given to him by the grand sophies of the Epicureans and Stoics than a sower of words,[2] a babbler (Acts 17:18). Would it not seem a strange opinion if one should assert that he who cleans the chariot is a better man than he who rides in it; that he who lives in a wilderness meanly clad and faring hardly is happier than they who are in king's houses and wear soft raiment; that he who is poor and is bid to sit at

---

1. *Christianus rustic as quam Alexander ethnicus.*
2. Σπερμολόγοι.

the footstool is more worthy than he who has the chief place given to him in the assembly? And can it sound less strange in the ears of the world that the most despicable condition of a believer is far above the happiness of him who has all the honors and delights that the earth can yield flowing in upon him, and meeting in him, as so many lines in one point?

I shall, therefore, endeavor to clear the truth of this inference so fully that it may serve to support and comfort afflicted Christians under all their pressures so as not to complain, because they are in their extremities happier than the best worlding in his delights; and that it may likewise provoke those who have made it their design to be great rather than good, to remind themselves of their folly, and to acknowledge that there is no tenure like an interest in the covenant and promises, and that there is no happiness like the happiness of a believer, which has its foundation laid in grace and not in greatness. To this end, let us in a few particulars compare or weigh, as in a balance, the worst of a believer's estate with the best of a worldly but yet a wicked man's estate, and we shall quickly see that the advantage will lie on that part of the scale in which the believer stands and not on the other.

Stranger in a Strange Land

First, a believer perhaps is in the world in no better condition than a stranger who has little or no interest in its enfranchisements, privileges, and immunities that others daily find the sweet of in the many benefits that they enjoy. He is frowned upon when others are courted and smiled upon by those who have honors and preferments in their power to bestow. He lives like Israel in Egypt, under hard pressures, when others rule and reign as lords. He is friendless and finds none either to pity his wrongs or to do him the least right. To his words, to his sighs, he finds a deaf and regardless ear continually turned when others have the law open, where they may implead their adversaries and have friends that are willing to countenance them and ready to help them. Can he, then, who lacks all these things be happier than he who enjoys them? Yes, for though a believer is a stranger here below, yet he is a citizen of the new Jerusalem that is above, to which every worldly man is a foreigner (Eph. 2:12). And from thence, He who bends His brow upon the wicked beholds him with love (Ps. 11:1–7). Though he is the world's bondman, yet he is the Lord's free man (1 Cor. 7:22). Though here he is friendless, yet what near and familiar relations have the whole blessed Trinity been pleased to take upon them, and to make known themselves by unto him? He has God as a Father, Christ as a Brother, and the Holy Spirit as a Comforter, all whom the men of the world can call by no such titles. Though here his supplications and his tears do not avail, yet in heaven his prayers are registered and his tears are bottled.

Having Few Possessions

Second, a believer, as he is a stranger, so also he may be afflicted with want, having little or nothing in possession to relieve his necessities. He may want clothing for his back and food for his belly. He may have only straw for his bed, grass and herbs for his meat when others sleep upon soft down and fare deliciously every day. He perhaps has scarcely enough water to quench his thirst when others have a variety of choice wines to please and delight their palates. All this and much more is acknowledged to be the lot and portion of many Christians, such of whom the world is not worthy. But yet let us view their condition so as to compare it with the men of the world whose bellies are filled with hidden treasure, and we shall quickly see that a true judgment and estimate being made of both that the thorns of the one will smell sweeter than the roses of the other. His necessities will be more desirable than their fullness because wants sanctified are better than unsanctified enjoyments. All their morsels are rolled up in the filth of their sin and in the bitterness of God's malediction; and all his wants are both sweetened and supplied with the comforts of God's promises. Though he has nothing for the present, yet he is rich in hopes. Though he has nothing in possession, yet he has an inheritance, a kingdom, a crown in reversion. They have all their good things in this life, and he has his reserved for the other. Though he has no food for his body, yet he has manna for his soul. He has a hungry body, and they have a starved soul. Though he has here scarcely a place to lay his head, yet is there room reserved for him in Abraham's bosom, where he shall forever dwell in joy when others lie down in sorrow (Isa. 50:10). Though his body is as a parched wilderness for thirst, yet his soul is as a watered garden, "Out of his belly shall flow rivers of living water" (John 7:38). We may truly say of a believer what Paul speaks of himself; though he was poor, yet he had enough to make many rich; though he had nothing, yet he possessed all things. To a Christian, all the world is his riches; to an unbeliever, not a dot of it. There is no creature that does not owe homage to Him, and shall certainly pay it, if his necessities require it. The heavens shall hear the earth, and the earth shall hear the corn and the wine and the oil in answer to Jezreel's prayers (Hos. 2:21–22). What is at further distance than the heavens, and so more unlikely to hear than the heavens? What creature is more dull than earth, and so more unfit to be affected and moved with a cry? And yet both the heavens and the earth shall not be deaf to Jezreel's prayers but shall fulfill their desires and supply their wants.

The Burden of Reproach

Third, a believer is not only exercised with the pressing evils of want and poverty, but he oftentimes lies under the sore burden of reproach and obloquy, which to an ingenuous spirit is more bitter than death itself. He is the common mark to which all the sharp arrows of men's tongues are directed. He is the only person that is taken up in the lips of talkers and is the infamy of the people (Ezek. 36:3), when others are in name as beautiful as Absalom, who from the sole of his foot to the crown of his head had no blemish in him; he is as Job on the dunghill, overspread with defamations that are as so many putrid ulcers. When others are cried up as the glory of their times, he is decried as the filth and offscouring of the world (1 Cor. 4:13). When the actions of others are blazoned as their virtues, his that are in themselves commendable are censured as full of pride, hypocrisy, affectation, and singularity. Where is then the blessedness of his condition that you spoke of? How can his estate that is overcast with a more pitchy darkness than that of the night be better than the best of theirs that has not the least shadow of any such evil stretching out itself upon it? It is true that none are more evil spoken of and blasted in their names than believers, but the ground of it does not spring from their just deserving but from the world's malice and enmity to God, which is derived to them for His sake. Let Nehemiah and the Jews set upon the rebuilding of the temple, and the repairing of the waste place of Jerusalem, and Sanballat upbraids them with intentions of rebellion (Neh. 6:6). Let Paul make known the gospel of Christ and the Jews who do not believe cry out that he is one of them who turns the world upside down (Acts 17:6). Let the primitive Christians who cannot safely meet in the day take the opportunity of the night to worship God; and let the heathens asperse their assemblies to be full of uncleanness and cruelty, and that they have suppers not much unlike that of Thiestes, king of Olympia, as Tertullian[3] shows in his apology for Christianity.[4]

---

3. Tertullian (155–220), early Christian apologist and Latin author; he wrote numerous tracts against heresies, including Gnosticism, and advanced the development of early Christian doctrine.

4. *Aplogeticum* (197).

Now, in these sufferings for God, there are such promises from God made and fulfilled to them that there is more sweetness to be found in the reproaches that they undergo for Him from the world than there can be contentment in its smiles or favor. And, therefore, Moses chose rather to suffer reproaches with Israel than to enjoy treasures in Egypt (Heb. 11:26). The contempt and slander they undergo on Christ's behalf serve both to make the present comforts sweeter and their reward hereafter more glorious. "Blessed are ye," said our Savior, "when men shall revile you, and persecute you, and shall say all manner of evil against you falsely, for my sake. Rejoice, and be exceeding glad: for great is your reward in heaven" (Matt. 5:11–12).

And now speak, O you worldlings, who judge happiness by as false a rule, as they do who measure their height by their shadow. Who is in a true estimate the better man, Elijah who runs before the chariot or Ahab who sits in it? John the Baptist, who is clothed with camels' hair, or Herod and his courtiers, who are arrayed with robes and costly garments? The poor whom God has chosen to be rich in faith and heirs of the kingdom (James 2:5), or the man that who the gold ring and the chief place in assemblies given unto him? Which condition is now more desirable, to be a stranger to the world and to be the Lord's free man, or to be an alien to God and the covenant of promise, and to be an inhabitant only of the world? To be rich to God and poor to men, or to be rich to men and poor to God? To be the favorite of heaven and be condemned on earth, or to be the darling of earth and the enemy of heaven? Oh, therefore, learn to judge happiness not by the light of sense but by the lamp of the sanctuary, and, in time, remind yourselves that nothing can be a foundation of happiness to you that has not its stability from the promise of God.

CHAPTER 20

Thankfulness for Precious Promises

A fourth application is to exhort believers that are made partakers of such great and precious promises to abound in all thankfulness to God and Christ, who are the sole fountain from whence these streams of living waters flow. When old Isaac had eaten of his son's venison, he blessed him that had prepared it for him. How much more should they that have tasted how good God is have their mouths filled with the blessing and praising of His name that has poured forth His love and mercy in such rich promises as are to the soul more sweet than marrow and fatness? To this duty, holy David quickens and stirs up himself when he summons all the faculties of his soul to praise the Lord: "All that is within me, bless his holy name" (Ps. 103:1). And that he may make the deeper impressions of God's goodness upon his own heart, he frames a short but yet a pithy compendium of His love towards him in His pardoning and healing grace, "Who forgiveth all thine iniquities; who healeth all thy diseases" (v. 3). In His redeeming and saving grace, He "redeemeth thy life from destruction," and "crowneth thee with lovingkindness and tender mercies" (v. 4). In His supporting and renewing mercies, He "satisfieth thy mouth with good things; so that thy youth is renewed like the eagle's" (v. 5). And of all these blessings are believers made partakers in the promises; it, therefore, becomes them to pay unto God a tribute of thankfulness, and that upon these grounds:

Grounds of Thankfulness

God's Chief End

First, the end of God's goodness to His creatures is His glory, and that which He chiefly delights in. Trumpeters love to sound where there is an echo; and God loves to bestow His mercies where He may hear of them again. For man to make the end of His actions in any kind to be His own praise does not only taint and fly-blow[1] His services with hypocrisy and pride so as to mar the beauty of them but also transforms them into vices that are hateful unto God and man. For it is not meet that he who derives his being from another should have his actions to terminate in himself. He that gives the being gives also the rule and end of its working, by both which the goodness of its actions are denominated. The rule of its working is the law and will of Him who gave it a being, and the end of all its actions is His glory. But God, who is the fountain of His own being, can have in all His works no other end than His own praise and glory. This is His end in all His works of creation: "The LORD hath made all things for himself" (Prov. 16:4). And this is the great end of all His works of grace in Christ: that we should be "to the praise of the glory of his grace" (Eph. 1:6). All the eternal purposes of God concerning man's salvation from the first to the last do ultimately resolve themselves into His glory.

Our Only Return

Secondly, to give unto God praise and thankful acknowledgments for His great and precious promises is all the return that we can make. David, as a man truly sensible of his many and deep obligations unto God, has a great consultation with himself,

---

1. *fly-blow*: corrupt.

which way he should express his thankfulness unto him: "What shall I render unto the LORD for all his benefits toward me?" (Ps. 116:12). But after all musings and studying with himself, he can find no other way but this: "I will take the cup of salvation, and call upon the name of the LORD" (v. 13). A Eucharistical sacrifice of praise and thanksgiving is all that David, though a king, can find to give unto God. And this kind of payment the poor may make as well as the rich, the young as well as the old. The children in the gospel can cry "Hosanna," and say, "Blessed is he that cometh in the name of the Lord" (Matt. 21:9), as well as others. It is a good observation of Nazianzen[2] that God has equalized all men in that ability which most recommends or discommends them unto Him, and that is the ability of the will to love Him and to give Him praise. This is that which all may do who have tasted how good God is, and this is all that the best can do who have been most filled with the riches of His mercy. Seeing, therefore, that a thankful recognition of God's love and bounty in His promises is the only recompense that we can make, it is most meet that we should abound in it, and make it not only the duty of our lips but of our hearts, breathing forth our very souls in the continual praises of Him who has manifested the gracious purposes of His heart unto us in many rich promises of life and salvation. More than this, God in His mercy does not desire; and less than this, in all reason we cannot give.

Heaven's Only Work

Thirdly, the giving of God praise and glory in endless songs of thanksgiving is the only work of the saints in heaven when fully made partakers of all the blessings that the promises hold

---

2. Gregory of Nazianzen (329–390), Bishop of Constantinople, and highly esteemed church father, known primarily for his orations and writings on pastoral theology.

forth. It is now the continual blessed exercise of all the inhabitants of those everlasting mansions in the highest heavens, and it shall be ours when we shall be translated thither, and have our faith turned into vision and our hope into enjoyment. Requisite, therefore, it is that what we know must be our eternal exercise in heaven to make that our frequent practice on earth.

Those persons that intend to travel into remote and foreign countries with an advantage unto themselves do beforehand acquaint themselves with the customs, manners, and fashions of the place to which they go, and from others whose experience may give the best light inquire what is the ingeny[3] and disposition of the natives, that so they may the better comply with their forms and civilities; yea, they endeavor to get some smattering of the language that they may not be altogether strangers to what is done and spoken there. So should Christians, who expect to dwell with the Lord forever, with all diligence inure themselves to the work and services of that innumerable company of angels and spirits of just men made perfect [Heb. 12:22–24], and to get some rudiments of their heavenly language while they are below that so they may the better bear a part in that celestial choir, singing with a loud voice, "Blessing, and glory, and wisdom, and thanksgiving, and honour, and power, and might, be unto our God for ever and ever" (Rev. 7:12).

Thankfulness Properly Expressed

Now that this duty of thankfulness may run in a right channel, I shall in some few particulars show how it may and ought to be expressed.

Holiness

First, let thankfulness appear in the fulfilling of that exhortation

---

3. *ingeny*: mind, intellect.

of the apostle, "Having therefore these promises, dearly beloved, let us cleanse ourselves from all filthiness of the flesh and spirit, perfecting holiness in the fear of God" (2 Cor. 7:1). The promises as they are causes working holiness, so also are they arguments inciting to it, being for the most part propounded as rewards unto the obedience of faith, which is a purifying and cleansing grace (Acts 15:9). In what more genuine fruits, therefore, can thankfulness manifest itself than in holiness? Or, how can a believer better evidence his high esteem of the promises than by his continual pressing forward to the perfection of sanctity? Now, as Aristotle tells us in the first book of his *Rhetoric*, that there are two ways by which men grow rich, either by adding to their present store[4] or else by subtracting and taking away from their expenses.[5] So also holiness is perfected by a double means: either by the addition of one grace unto another, which is the duty that Saint Peter calls for, "Add to your faith virtue; and to virtue knowledge; and to knowledge temperance; and to temperance patience; and to patience godliness" (2 Peter 1:5–6), or else by not making provision for the flesh, to fulfill the lusts thereof, which is the counsel that Saint Paul gives to believers (Rom. 13:14). And he that does not [in] both [of] these ways endeavor [for] the increase of holiness, starving the boundless desires of the flesh and strengthening the graces of the Spirit by renewing acts of godliness, can never be rich either in grace or comfort.

Witness

Secondly, let thankfulness for the promises be expressed in proclaiming that mercy [and] salvation and assured peace, which you have received from them. If so be you have tasted that God is good, do as the birds, which when they come to a full heap,

---

4. πρὸς τὰ ὑπάρχοντα προστιθέντες.
5. τῶν δαπανημάτων ἀφαιρούντες.

chirp and invite their fellows. Tell the hungry soul what satisfying and blessed food the promises are: the dejected, what reviving cordials; the poor, what enduring riches; the broken and wounded, what healing balsams they are; that so they may be encouraged to take hold of these promises by a hand of faith.

Cripples that return with health from the bath hang up their crutches on the trees and their rags on the hedges that are near that thereby they may win credit and esteem to the waters. And so, to honor the wells of salvation, should Christians make known the great things that God has done for them, and leave in every place where they come some testimony of their thankfulness and God's goodness. "Come and hear," says David, "all ye that fear God, and I will declare what he hath done for my soul" (Ps. 66:16).

He does not call them, as Augustine observes, to acquaint them with speculations [as to] how wide the earth is, how far the heavens are stretched out, what the number of the stars is, or what is the course of the sun, but come and I will tell you the wonders of His grace, the faithfulness of His promises, the riches of His mercy to my soul. Oh! that believers would be persuaded to declare thus the experiences that they have any time had of God's truth and power in His Word, and in a way of gratitude to communicate them unto others. How instrumental might they thereby become in the comforting and establishing of others? Experiences are like milk in the breast of the nurse that has received a concoction and is thereby made a more facile and pure nourishment to the child that partakes of it.

Blessing
Thirdly, let thankfulness for the precious promises be expressed in a most affectionate blessing of God for the Lord Jesus Christ, by whom all that is wrapped up in them is given unto us. He is the first matter, as it were, out of which God has framed all

our good. He is the receptacle in which all blessings are laid up, and the Well-head from whence they all flow. By His blood, the promises are purchased for us, and by His most powerful intercession, they are made good unto us. Alas! how little efficacy would all our prayers have, if they were not presented to God the Father by His hand? How small acceptance would our persons find, if God did not look upon us in Him? How uncertain would all our comforts be, if the root of them were not in Him, if He were not as the tree of life upon which they grow? Yea, how quickly should we spy a hell that might amaze us between heaven and any other ground of confidence that could possibly be imagined by us out of Christ. When, therefore, we do at any time make a thankful recognition of God's goodness to us in the particular mercies of the promises of the gospel, let us be sure to put the name of Christ to all. When we bless God for blotting out our iniquities, for pardoning freely all our sins, let us set this crown upon the head of the mercy: that He has done it in Christ. When we bless Him for sanctifying us, let us ever add for His sanctifying us in Christ. When we praise Him for our adoption and sonship, let us bless Him for doing it in Christ. When we honor Him for the assured hopes of life and glory in heaven, let us say, as the apostle does, "Blessed be the God and Father of our Lord Jesus Christ, who hath blessed us with all spiritual blessings in heavenly places in Christ" (Eph. 1:3).

Anticipation

Fourthly, let thankfulness for the promises appear in strong desires, and vehement pantings after the plenary possession and perfect enjoyment of all that felicity of which they are the earnests and pledges given us by God. In this life, we are but as kings in the cradle, the setting of the crown upon our heads is reserved till we come to heaven. Here we are but as espoused persons, and not as the bride in her best clothes; in the other life, we put on the robes of glory, which shall make our bodies shine ten thousand times brighter than the sun, and our souls ten thousand times brighter than our bodies. Here, we are but as invited guests to the feast and supper of the great King; we sit not down at His table till we come to heaven, and then Christ bids us eat, "O friends, and drink abundantly, O beloved." While, therefore, we are absent from the Lord, and do by the eye of faith only peep into the things that are within the veil, and enjoy a few foretastes of glory and immortality, we should show how highly we prize the promises by longing after and wishing for the final accomplishment of all. Oh! when will it be that I shall see Him in whose blood I was washed, by whose stripes I was healed, by whose Spirit I was sanctified, by whose merits such great things are prepared for me? How long, Lord, holy and true, will it be ere death shall be swallowed up in victory, and mortality put on immortality? Thus Bernard, upon those words of our Savior ("A little while, and ye shall not see me: and again, a little while, and ye shall see me" [John 16:16]), passionately expresses himself: "Good Lord, dost Thou call that a little while in which I shall not see Thee? O long, long little!"[6] Such desires as these are true evidences of a thankful heart.

---

6. *Pie Domine, modicum illud vocas in quo te non videam? O modicum, modicum longum!*

CHAPTER 21

Motive to Act Faith in the Promises

The fifth and last application is to stir up believers to act "precious faith" (2 Peter 1:1), as the apostle calls it, upon the precious promises, without which what are the promises in the Word, but as sugar in the wine that lying unstirred does not sweeten; but as full breasts undrawn that do not nourish; but as beds of spices that, being unblown upon, do not lend forth their fragrant and delightful odors? It is the exercise and skill of faith that fetches out the virtue and sweetness which lies hid in them, as it is the industry of the bee that extracts the honey from the flowers. The bee would starve notwithstanding all the flowery meadows, if it did not labor; and so would a Christian languish and pine away notwithstanding all the precious promises, if faith should be idle and inactive. O, then, that I might prevail with believers to cast aside every weight that hinders, and to set on work this noble and divine grace of faith, whose glory and worth is not to be seen in the habit but in the acts of it. What does Samson differ from another man while he sleeps in the lap of Delilah? But when he awakes out of his sleep, and breaks the withs and cords that bound him, as a thread of towe[1] when it touches the fire, and carries away the beam and the web in which his locks are

---

1. *towe*: rope.

fastened, then his strength appears in its greatness to be matchless. And so, in what is a believer distinguished from another man while the habit of faith lies asleep in his bosom, and is not actuated on the promises? But when it stirs, and rouses up itself to take hold of God and Christ in His Word, how apparent is the strength of the one, and the weakness of the other made to every eye? What burdens does the one stand under and carry away upon his shoulders under which the other sinks? What temptations does the one overcome, unto which the other without resistance yields? What viper does the one shake off his hand into the fire without the least hurt, which fasten upon the other, and sting him unto death? It is faith which makes us to rejoice in tribulations (Rom. 5:3). It is faith which makes us to possess our souls in patience in fiery trials (Heb. 10:36). It is faith which makes us resolute in desertions (Jonah 2:4). It is faith which makes every condition of life comfortable (Hab. 2:4).

But that I may yet more fully prosecute this exhortation which hitherto is as a vessel upon the wheel of the potter that has not received its perfect shape, I shall propound some particular arguments and considerations that may animate believers to live the life of faith, which stands chiefly in two things. First, in a knowledge of, and a familiar acquaintance with the Word, so as to have it in readiness for direction. Secondly, in a right improvement and exercise of faith on the Word and promises of God. For as faith is truly the life and guide of the soul, so the Word is the ground, life, and guide of our faith. Now, the arguments that I shall set down are briefly three.

It Is God's Design

First, the life of faith is that life which above all others God would have believers to live. And this appears by the distance that God has put between His promises and His performances, making their whole life to be rather a life of hopes than of enjoyments, and the good things that He gives to relate more to the future than to the present time. God was graciously pleased to open a door of hope to fallen man in that first gospel promise which He Himself proclaimed, that the seed of the woman should break the serpent's head (Gen. 3:15). But how many generations passed away before the fullness of time came, in which He sent forth His Son made of a woman? He has promised to believers that they shall tread down the wicked, and that they shall be ashes under the soles of their feet (Mal. 4:3). But yet He has made their warfare to be as long as their life. He has promised a glorious resurrection of their bodies out of the grave, and yet for how many thousand years have His saints lain dissolved in their dust, as if they did seem to be altogether forgotten by Him? Now, to what end has God set such long periods of time between the making and the accomplishing of His promises? But only that He would have the heirs of them to live by faith; yea, and to die in faith by resting on the truth of His Word for the fulfilling of every mercy which He has undertaken for in His promises. And indeed this glory which believers give to God in the exercise of their faith upon His Word is far greater, and more noble, than all that glory which the whole universe of creatures yield unto Him. They give Him the glory of His goodness in their being, and in the comforts of it derived unto them by Him. But who gives Him the glory of His faithfulness in His promises but a believer? Who is it that rejoices "in hope of the glory of God" (Rom. 5:2) but a believer? Who glories in tribulations but a believer? Who is it that lets not his confidence die when his life expires but a believer? "My flesh and my heart faileth," says David, "but God is the strength[2] of my heart, and my portion for ever" (Ps. 73:26).

---

2. Spurstowe has "rock."

It Is Most Delightful

Secondly, the life of faith is of all estates the most contented, and of all lives the fullest of real sweetness and delight.

Contentment

First, it is the most contented life. True contentment is the inseparable companion of true faith (1 Tim. 6:6). A believer is the only person that is instructed in this sacred mystery (Phil. 4:11–13). The things that others want, he desires not. Riches, which others covet with the straining of their consciences, he throws away as snares. Pleasures, which others drink down with a thirst unsatisfied, he out of choice sparingly sips of, or else refuses so much as to taste. Honors that others value themselves by, he looks upon as fancies and not realities. As Plato told the musicians, that a philosopher could dine and eat his meat without them, so a believer can live happily without having any of these things. And the ground of all this is because by faith he lives above them, and enjoys more high and noble delights in the very expectation and hope of that blessedness which God has promised than any other can have from the fruition of an earthly paradise, or of the whole world itself, if turned and changed into an Eden.

Sweetness

Secondly, of all lives, the life of faith is the sweetest. The delicacies that faith feeds upon do not arise from any stagnant and impure pits or cisterns but from the fountain and well of life. It sucks the breasts of consolation (Isa. 66:11). It lives upon the free favor of God, which is better than life itself (Ps. 63:3). It has Christ himself for nutriment, whose flesh is meat indeed, whose blood is drink indeed (John 6:55). All [of] which are food the world knows not of; it never understood their preciousness, or tasted their sweetness. There is a greater difference between the repasts of faith, and the refreshments of the world, than there is between the physic of the Galenists and Paracelsians, the one giving it in the drug, and the other, as they boast, in the quintessence and spirits extracted from that phlegm and earthy matter that deadens and allays their efficacy. All the comforts of faith have in them a native purity and spiritualness, and need not the help of artists to refine them. Such they are, as that angels themselves have neither better nor higher to live upon. How injurious, then, are believers to their own happiness while they neglect the living by faith, and gaze rather upon these dainties with their eyes, than feed upon them with their mouths? How greatly do they live below themselves while they take up with the things of this world, and put not forth this divine grace of faith, which can fetch every good thing out of heaven? What dishonor do they cast on the precious promises while like the lustful Israelites they slight this manna of the gospel as dry food? O, therefore, if there be any consolation in Christ, if any comfort of love, if any fellowship of the Spirit, if any excellency in the promises, be persuaded, you that are the beloved ones of God, to live the life of faith, and to exercise it in an improvement of the promises, the use of which makes you more rich and blessed than having them.

It Is Most Sure

Thirdly, to move believers to act faith upon the promises, I shall add this argument, that their labor and expectation will not be in vain. Faith in the promise is like the bow of Jonathan, and the sword of Saul, which never returned empty (2 Sam. 1:22). It always finds what it seeks, and enjoys what it desires. "He that believeth on him shall not be confounded" (1 Peter 2:6); that is, he shall not be disappointed or broken in his purposes or hopes. If the promise be not good security to rest and build upon, what is? What bond can be so firm as His Word, who "cannot lie"

(Titus 1:2)? What pledge can be more certain than the earnest of the Spirit, by which the inheritance of believers is sealed unto them (Eph. 1:14)? If these foundations fail, then we may well say with the prophet, "What can the righteous do?" But sooner shall the rocks be broken into bits, and thrown as pebbles, and cockleshells upon the shore by the violence of the waves; sooner shall the mountains that God has set fast by His strength (Ps. 65:6) be overturned by the breath of tempestuous winds than the promises which are founded upon the immutable power of God and the never-failing goodness of Christ be in the least iota made void and of no effect. For besides the infallibility of God's Word, which may abundantly confirm unto believers the truth of the promises, the goodness also and mercy of Christ are as another sacred anchor for their faith and confidence to rest upon, if, in relation to the promises, it be seriously thought on in two particulars.

The Purchase of Christ

First, that the promises are the real purchase of the precious blood of Christ, and must therefore be certainly made good, or else He must be a loser in all His sufferings. If He, like Jonathan (1 Sam. 18:4), should strip Himself not only of His robes but of His life that He might express His love to distressed and undone persons, with whom God is angry and displeased, and yet they receive no advantage or fruit by it, would not all these condescensions of goodness and mercy be in vain? If He should drink of that brook and torrent of curses that was in the way between salvation and sinners, and yet the passage to the heavenly Canaan be no more open than it was before, should not Christ be a greater loser than sinners themselves? They, it is true, lose their souls, each of which are of more value than so many worlds, but Christ must lose the revenue of His glory, which is far more precious than the souls of all the men in the world.

How would sin exult and triumph, if it should ever be able to say there was a pardon covenanted for to be given such a person, but I have hindered the execution of it? How would Satan reproach the death of Christ, if he could be able to say that he has destroyed one soul for whom Christ died? Yea, how should Paul, or any other believer be able to throw forth their gantlet, and to challenge all the enemies of salvation to do their worst (Rom. 8:31), if any of them could make a separation between the love of Christ and them? How quickly would tribulation, persecution, famine, [and] nakedness say we will make you miserable? How soon would perils and the sword reply we will conquer you? How confidently would principalities and powers say we will pluck you out of Christ's hand? But forever blessed be His name, there are none among the whole host of enemies that dare revile the confidence of a believer, or say as that uncircumcised Philistine to David, "I will give thy flesh unto the fowls of the air, and to the beasts of the field" (1 Sam. 17:44). There are none that dare presume to say that they can make void the least mercy which the promise holds forth to be the gift of Christ's love, and the purchase of His blood. Let, therefore, believers lift up the hands which hang down, and put forth the strength of faith in renewed acts of confidence upon the promises, being fully persuaded in themselves of this truth, that they can no more be disappointed of their hopes than Christ can be disappointed of His purchase.

The Intercession of Christ

Secondly, that the promises are the matter of the most prevailing intercession of Christ, who now sits on the right hand of God in glory. When He was on earth, He purchased, by the price of His blood, all that mass of treasure and riches both of grace and glory that are inventoried in the promises, and by His last will and testament on the cross bequeathed them to believers. But all this which was transacted here below was only, as divines usually term it, the means of procurement,[3] or obtaining it for believers; the means of applying all this unto them[4] are as His resurrection and intercession: His resurrection that declares His conquest over death; His intercession that shows His favor and acceptance with God. And they are both as necessary to make His satisfaction of force unto believers as the image or stamp of the prince is to make the coin currant, though it neither add weight or value to the substance. He, says the apostle, "being made perfect, he became the author of eternal salvation unto all them that obey him" (Heb. 5:9).

Now, the intercession of Christ is set forth in Scripture with all the advantages that may be, that thereby believers may be secured of their interest and title to the things which He has purchased: "We have a great high priest, that is passed into the heavens, Jesus the Son of God, let us hold fast our profession" (Heb. 4:14). First, He is a great High Priest, greater than all that were before Him, both in power and favor with God. Secondly, He is passed into the heavens, a sanctuary which no other priest could ever enter into, or sit down in, all their sacrifices being imperfect and therefore to be daily renewed by them. Thirdly, He is Jesus, the Son of God, more near in alliance unto Him than angels or men, and therefore most sure to prevail for the obtaining of whatever He asks or requires of Him.

When He, therefore, who is the only favorite of heaven is the believer's advocate and continually solicits God to fulfill His covenant made with Him, and His people's prayers made unto Him, what ground can there be for jealousies and distrust in a believer's heart? What rational impediment can there be imagined to hinder or weaken the confidence of faith, which

---

3. *medium impetrationis.*
4. *medium applicationis.*

the intercession of Christ does not fully remove and take away? Are your prayers tainted with the corruption and infirmities of the flesh? He perfumes them with the sweet odors of His intercession (Rev. 8:3). Are your sins multiplied and renewed daily? So are the intercessions of Christ; it is His only work in heaven to intercede for sinners (Heb. 7:25). Are your persons vile, and such which you fear God will not accept? Christ, who is your High Priest, is holy, harmless, and separate from sinners (Heb. 7:26). He has in His person a fullness of all perfections, which may assure every believer that the promises which He pleads, that the requests which He makes to God in Christ's name, shall not be like arrows shot at the sun, which never reach it, or come near to it; but that they shall pierce the heavens, and be of such power and prevalency with God, as that what they seek, He will grant, and the promises which they plead in faith, He will perform and make good in truth. Wherefore, let me again commend unto believers the great duty of exercising faith on the promises of Christ, which cannot but fill the heart with strong and inseparable consolations, when, by the eye of faith, they are looked upon as those great things, which are both the purchase of His most precious blood, and the matter of His most powerful intercession.

Conclusion

And now as mariners, who, when they come nigh the port, roll up their sails which were before spread, they being not useful in the harbor that were before most necessary on the sea. So must I, being arrived at that point which was the utmost boundary of my thoughts and intentions, draw towards a conclusion, and wind up this whole discourse concerning the excellency and the use of the promises of the gospel, which has hitherto been dilated and insisted on in the several particulars. And yet, methinks, I had need to wish new sides, new lungs, and a hour new turned up, that I might begin all again, or else to sit down and complain with the prophet, "I have laboured in vain, I have spent my strength for nought" (Isa. 49:4). O, where are those affectionate expressions, acclamations, and rejoicings of heart, which I expected would have echoed from every mouth and have appeared in every face that had heard and been acquainted with such glad tidings of peace and mercy as the promises declare and testify from heaven towards sinners? I had thought that some as full of heavenly admiration would have stood like the cherubims, with bowed heads, and faces looking towards the mercy-seat, as being desirous to pry and search more into these divine mysteries which are the delightful study of angels. That others, like Peter in the mount of transfiguration, having had some glimpses of the glory of heaven, would have cried out, "It is good being here." Or wish, as David, "that I may dwell in the house of the LORD all the days of my life, to behold the beauty of the LORD" (Ps. 27:4)! I had thought that others, at the opening of these wells of salvation, and a free invitation to drink of these waters, which whosoever drinks of shall never thirst again, would, like the woman of Samaria, have said, "Sir, give me this water, that I thirst not, neither come hither to draw" (John 4:15). That others at the gathering of this manna, which has been plentifully rained down upon them, and gives life beyond death, would with most sincere hearts have made that prayer which the Jews did in hypocrisy, "Lord, evermore give us this bread" (John 6:34); but alas! "who hath believed our report? and to whom hath the arm of the Lord been revealed?" (John 12:38). Methinks, still men stand altogether unaffected, as if this day salvation had not been brought, either to their houses, or to their hearts, as if nothing had been spoken that concerned their everlasting happiness. They are like Paul's auditory that heard him preach of the resurrection of Christ: some scorn, others doubt, and few believe (Acts 17). Brethren, from whence is it, I beseech you, that there is so little change and alteration made either in your countenances or in your affections? Is it because I have shown you the glory and preciousness of the promises only through a crevice, which you would willingly have beheld with open face? Alas! who is it that can see these things in their luster and live? You can never understand their worth, till you come to enjoy them in heaven. Or, is it because this treasure is brought unto you in an earthen vessel that you set so low a value upon it? God it is who has so ordered the dispensation that the excellency of the power may be of God, and not of us (2 Cor. 4:7). Or, do you expect that I should heap up more arguments that might further commend the promises unto you? O, how easily, as well as gladly, could I undertake this task, if that I might be but sure to endear the promises to you thereby? Diodorus[1] tells of a city in Sicilia that was called Triocala because it had springs of water of a superlative sweetness, vineyards of the choicest wine, and rocks of most impregnable strength. But how much more truly may the promises of the gospel be styled not Triocala but Pancala, which are not only as overflowing well-springs of living water, nor as pleasant vineyards that abound with wine that makes glad the heart, nor as insuperable rocks against which the gates of hell are never able to prevail, but are also a celestial Eden, in which, as Bernard pithily [says], "there is everything that you would desire, and nothing that you would dislike."[2] But I may not forget myself, and instead of casting anchor in the haven, spread the canvas, and put forth to sea again. I shall, therefore, cease from speaking to you, and shall turn all my expostulations with you into prayers to God for you, beseeching Him who in Paul's planting, and Apollo's watering, alone gives the increase; that He would by the mighty working of His Holy Spirit make what has been spoken to be a word of effectual grace unto you that have heard it, that it may build you up, and give you an inheritance among all them that are sanctified. And that He would vouchsafe the same blessing to all those that by His providence may now read what others have heard; that so His name to whom alone all is due may have the whole praise and the glory.

---

1. Diodorus of Sicily (1st century BC), Greek historian and author of *Bibliotheca historica*, a massive universal history of the ancient world.

2. *totum quod velis, et nihil quod nolis.*